A Simple Guide to

Upgrading and repairing PCs

E. Charton

Prentice Hall Europe

London New York Toronto Sydney Tokyo Singapore Madrid
Mexico City Munich Paris

First published in 1998 as Entretien et dépannage du PC
– Se Former en 1 Jour by
Simon & Schuster Macmillan (France)
This edition published 1999 by
Prentice Hall Europe
An imprint of
Pearson Education Limited
Edinburgh Gate
Harlow
Essex CM20 2JE, England

© 1997 Simon & Schuster Macmillan (France)
19, rue Michel Le Comte
75003 Paris
France

Translated by Berlitz Translation Services UK, Baldock, Hertfordshire

Printed and bound in Great Britain by
Redwood Books, Trowbridge, Wiltshire

Library of Congress Cataloging-in-Publication Data

Available from the publisher

British Library Cataloguing in Publication Data

A catalogue record for this book is available from the British Library
ISBN 0-13-021240-7

1 2 3 4 5 03 02 01 00 99

Table of Contents

PART II: Starting again from scratch

Introduction

Have you ever come across an unexplained error when using your PC? Have you ever found that, for no obvious reason, your computer starts to make worrying noises, slows down or even stops working altogether? The answer is almost certainly "yes"! The daily life of a PC user can be full of mini-disasters which detract from the pleasure of working on a PC.

Furthermore, there are problems which often follow modifications and installation of software or peripherals. For example, "Ever since I installed the 'whatsit' card, I constantly get 'register base' errors." Or, "I installed the latest version of the DirectX 5.0 driver. Now, when I run the REDLINE game, it starts up, but the display starts to flicker." These are samples of the dozens of calls received each day by technical support services.

From the outset, the PC has had an (unfortunately justified) bad reputation: constantly prone to error, difficult to configure, hard to keep up and running and sometimes incomprehensible to the point where some users come to hate their machine.

However, it is worth noting that although, for historical reasons, your computer is made in such a way that it will always be subject to minor faults, this does not mean that these will inevitably lead to a complete breakdown or that you should resign yourself to the problem, hoping that your PC will miraculously right itself.

It is possible to use your PC under good working conditions and to make light of minor problems simply by observing a few rules for good management of your PC, and having a basic understanding of electronic maintenance. With a PC, it is important to prevent, maintain, manage and anticipate. Following a few simple rules, and some straightforward, easy-to-implement advice is usually enough to maintain a PC in top condition. The objective of this book is to teach users how to maintain their PCs with minimum effort.

Action

This book sets out the rules for maintaining a PC. As with a car, a PC will require routine maintenance and repair as follows:

- it will be necessary, from time to time, to change the operating system and the drivers;

- it will be necessary to delete old files which are no longer needed; and

- in the worst case, if your PC breaks down, repair may not be possible and you may need to start again from scratch.

With practice, you will find that these procedures are not too complicated. The tasks which a user should perform to maintain a PC in top condition are summarised below.

- **Configuring:** indicating to the computer, or to the software, which parameters must be used in order for your PC to run efficiently. Configuration is usually carried out via menus and check-boxes.

- **Installation:** adding new software or peripherals, ensuring that software programs are always operational and that the installation is error-free and complete.

- **Uninstalling:** deleting software, files or peripherals which are no longer needed, leaving the fewest possible remaining files.

- **Updating:** checking at regular intervals that software programs are error-free and that there are no new versions or "patches" which might solve certain unexplained problems, and making sure that the driver for peripherals (such as a printer, modem, or scanner) is up-to-date.

- **Cleaning:** deleting anything in the PC which is no longer required: old files or drivers, unneeded software, using specialised cleaning utilities to search for "garbage" which would not otherwise be found.

- **Repairs:** the PC user should be able to carry out minor repair work without the need of advice from a dealer.

If the above measures are carried out, your PC will be able to operate efficiently and speedily and unexplained errors will be kept to a minimum.

THE CONTENTS OF THIS BOOK

During the course of 12 chapters, each of which can be covered in an hour, we will consider the working of a PC. In Part 1, the first nine hours, you will learn how to manage and maintain a computer on a day-to-day basis:

- **Hour 1** is theoretical: understanding the causes so that you can later implement the solutions.

- **Hour 2** is educational: describing basic dealings with your PC on the basis that prevention is better than cure.

- **Hour 3** discusses tidying up the hard disk using the utilities which are already available on your computer.

- **Hour 4** and **Hour 5** cover installing/uninstalling software and saving space: a congested disk will result in a system which is more difficult to use.

- **Hour 6** and **Hour 7** are devoted to updating drivers and updating your system should you wish to progress to the latest version of an operating system.

- **Hour 8** discusses viruses and explains how to eliminate them.

- **Hour 9** provides advice for when all else fails.

Part 2, **Hours 10** to **12**, applies to extreme cases and demonstrate how to start from scratch and produce a PC in top condition: from preparatory work, through formatting, to system installation.

SPECIAL ICONS

In this book, in addition to the text and figures, you will find items which emphasize certain points.

These notes provide additional information about the subject concerned.

These notes indicate a variety of shortcuts: keyboard shortcuts, 'Wizard' options, techniques reserved for experts, etc.

These notes warn you of the risks associated with a particular action and, where necessary, show you how to avoid any pitfalls.

A FEW QUESTIONS AND ANSWERS

Q Why isn't the PC "naturally" in tip-top condition?

A This is due to the history of the PC: explanations can be found in Hour 1.

Q What is a file allocation error?

A See Hour 3.

Q How do you remedy mysterious Windows errors?

A See Hours 3 and 7.

Q Is it necessary to uninstall items which are no longer needed?

A See Hour 4.

Q How do I tidy up my hard disk?

A See Hour 3.

Q My Windows system is locked up: what should I do?

A See Hour 2.

Q How do I check whether my drivers are up-to-date?

A See Hour 6.

Q Can Windows be updated? What is the advantage of this?

A See Hour 7.

Part 1

Rules for correct use

Hour 1

General survey

THE CONTENTS FOR THIS HOUR

- The causes of poor PC performance
- The difference between "failure" and "configuration"
- Sources of problems

Before studying in detail the day-to-day actions which will help you to work happily on your PC, it is useful to reflect on why there is a need for this book.

In 90% of cases, responsibility for the poor running of a computer does not lie with the manufacturer or the dealer or the supplier of accessories or software, or even with the reliability of the hardware: it is the PC's history that has made it such a fragile tool.

THE CAUSES OF POOR PC PERFORMANCE

The inventor of your computer, whatever its make, is IBM. This manufacturer, in settling upon an "open" computer, the IBM PC, sowed the seeds which gave birth to the PC industry as we know it today. Here is a brief summary of the characteristics of this historic computer:

- it is "open", i.e. it can accommodate accessories for which it was not necessarily designed, such as sound cards, modems, etc.;

- its intelligence is not fixed: in other words, the operating system with which it is equipped (Windows 95, Windows 98 or any other system) can be modified and improved over the years;

- it is upwards compatible: when you change PC, you can use your old software and peripherals on your new machine; and

- copying of the IBM PC is authorised by its manufacturer: thousands of manufacturers will soon, therefore, be producing "compatible" machines.

These four points explain the success of IBM-compatible PCs. They also point to the causes of malfunctions in your computer:

- "open" means thousands of manufacturers capable of producing thousands of accessories which are not always compatible with one another;

- an "open-ended" and "compatible" system means that Windows is intended to work on millions of potentially quite different machines;

- "standard" and "evolution" mean that the PC is not to be thrown away every year which, in turn, means that it may be important to update software programs or add new ones; and

- "compatible" means that each PC is designed according to a different specification by different manufacturers in order to achieve the same result everywhere ... at least, in theory.

A vast assortment of "standard" PCs
PCs, irrespective of their manufacturer, are very different computers, made up of different accessories, and yet are all compatible with one another: this is what is meant by "standard".

This standard is continually changing and therefore creates an infinite number of minor variations which are liable to disrupt the life of your computer.

The first step, therefore, is to learn to tell the difference between a failure, which is inevitably caused by hardware, and a malfunction, which is almost always due to software. You will often encounter the term "instability" for describing this state of erratic operation.

You should realise that a PC that works poorly, behaves bizarrely or produces incomprehensible errors (i.e. which is "unstable") has not, strictly speaking, failed. It simply needs maintenance and updating.

Figure 1.1: The PC is an assembly of assorted peripherals. This means thousands of drivers which must be made to work together!

THE DIFFERENCE BETWEEN "FAILURE" AND "CONFIGURATION"

Accustomed as we are to call in a plumber for a water leak, the gas company when we smell gas and an electrician when there's no power, we often think that any electronic device which is working incorrectly has failed. Our instinct is to call in a repair man.

Consequently, when a PC starts to make worrying noises, the temptation is to refer to the manufacturer or the dealer, who generally want nothing to do with it or have no time for sorting out what they see as a simple "configuration problem".

However, although for a number of us the PC is so mysterious that a simple whirring is the symptom of a serious problem, this is not necessarily the case. A hard disk which slows down is almost always a problem of everyday maintenance or use. It may also be due to system errors which have accumulated, likewise visual or functional faults: configuration can have an effect on all these things.

The PC is unlike anything else in your everyday environment. You should learn a minimum number of routine maintenance actions in order to use it comfortably. It is a matter of distinguishing a "failure", which is likely to necessitate the action of a professional, from a "malfunction" which you are perfectly capable of rectifying yourself.

You have all the tools for rectifying malfunctions by configuring and maintaining your PC. What is more, no service company will ever maintain a PC on your behalf. You must therefore prepare yourself and learn to recognise what is wrong with your machine.

What you can rectify and improve yourself

We will begin with the symptoms of the problem, which tell us a lot about its causes.

- Do not rely on appearances: contrary to all expectations, text which does not display correctly on-screen, or a peripheral (modem or sound card) which runs slowly , or perhaps not at all, seldom means that an accessory has failed, but instead that it is being incorrectly managed by your system and is therefore incorrectly installed or configured.

- A hard disk which indicates "error on track xxx, lost sectors" is not a symptom of failure, but a sign of incorrect configuration or a maintenance fault on the hard disk.

- A PC which doesn't start up and displays error messages of the type "boot impossible" or "hard disk inaccessible" is the sign of a serious operating problem, but seldom of a peripheral fault. You have the tools to rectify this type of problem.

- When Windows 95 displays "fault in module XXX", this means without any doubt that the system lacks stability as a result of lack of cleaning, rather than a hardware fault.

- If a software program causes the machine to crash, possibly followed by a black screen, it is almost always due to a configuration or maintenance fault, rarely a failure.

Figure 1.2: Spectacular error messages are rarely symptomatic of a hardware failure

Admittedly, the above are examples of spectacular symptoms that a PC is not in top condition, but these can be rectified and anticipated. This is not to say that the PC is infallible and that the hardware never breaks down. Generally these problems exist because, in order to make their applications work on the widest possible range of equipment, the software publishers and hardware manufacturers perform programming feats which simply cannot guarantee "zero fault".

Then again, genuine failures do occur.

Problems for the professional

Physical breakdowns of a PC really are occasional, much rarer than those of a television or washing machine, for example.

My experience as an author could be enlightening on this subject. I have worked on PCs since 1986 and have personally used around 15 different PCs.

- My two Amstrad 1512 PCs from 1986 are still working, including the hard disks and network cards.

- One of the VGA video cards from my first 386 PC in 1989 is installed on a 486 DX and is still working today.

- After ten years of using PCs, no motherboard has ever failed.

- The only genuine failures encountered during this period relate to a poor quality hard disk, mounted on a 286 PC (failed in 1989), an Artisoft network card and a USR modem, put out of action by a voltage surge during a thunderstorm!

I should add that two of the machines which I tested during this period actually broke down. A Tandon PC processor "burned out" and an IBM Treka portable LCD screen stopped working. They were, however, two pilot production machines. Furthermore, Tandon no longer exists, and IBM quickly ceased production of the machines in question.

Experience has therefore shown that PCs and their peripherals meet a remarkable manufacturing quality. Only the following symptoms could be genuine signs of failure:

- several beeps at start-up and a black screen;

- a hard disk light which remains permanently on;

- strange characters being displayed at start-up; and

- no result on power-up (in this case always check that the power plug is actually plugged in).

For these problems, unfortunately, this book can do nothing.

SOURCES OF PROBLEMS

We will now examine the various peripherals of a PC, those which, incorrectly configured, badly maintained, or poorly managed, may lead to problems in a PC.

The hard disk: the nerve centre of a PC

We will start with the most sensitive item, the hard disk. This peripheral performs several functions, most obviously storage of information. A hard disk contains your files and the applications which generated them, but this is not its only function. The hard disk also contains your operating system and a multitude of hidden information which allows the PC to recognise and manage the hard disk, as well as the files and applications stored on it. This hidden information is often involved in many crisis situations. It comprises:

- "manufacturing" information relating to the physical characteristics of the medium. The manufacture of a hard disk is a complex process, and this industrial process can produce "errors", that is, create areas of the disk which are unusable. Although this is entirely normal, it is essential to indicate to the software the position of these areas so that they are not used. If they were, the applications would record errors. This information is generated by means of so-called "basic" formatting. We will come back to this. For now it is enough to say that the Windows 95 ScanDisk utility or the Windows 3.x CHKDSK utility are the tools responsible for rectifying this type of problem.

- hidden information concerning the letter of the disk (C, D, E, etc.) and its mode of operation (start-up when the machine is powered up). This information is managed by the FDISK tool to which we will also return.

- "structural" information which is created by formatting: a hard disk is formatted exactly like a diskette. In fact, on leaving the factory, the disk is only a "potentially free" space. In order to make it usable, it is necessary to organise it for an operating system: just as if you drew columns and lines on a blank sheet to organise your data. It is the FORMAT command which organises a hard disk. A deficient format, as a result of a virus attack or a software fault for example, may be the source of problems on a PC.

- hidden information which relates to the many temporary files used by applications software or operating systems. In fact, each software program sometimes needs to store, temporarily, information essential to its operation. These files, which theoretically exist only when the software is used, are supposed to disappear as soon as the program is closed. The reality sometimes differs from this theory.

The above constitute the "system" information. It goes without saying that problems occur if this system data is not completely up-to-date, operational and organised. However, a hard disk may work incorrectly for other reasons, for example:

- if it is cluttered up with a multitude of files which are no longer needed;

- if it is attacked by a virus; or

- when a faulty software program has destroyed part of its content.

We will examine all these points in the following hours. However, the hard disk is not the only possible cause of operating problems. The drivers and operating system may also cause errors.

System and driver version problems

Your PC is a heterogeneous assembly, a multitude of pieces of hardware assembled to form a coherent whole. Here, a card for the printer, there, another for displaying on the screen. In order to make this assembly homogeneous, the PC uses an "operating system", Windows 95 or Windows NT, for example, associated with drivers, small sections of program which serve as interfaces between the peripherals and the applications.

The operation of the "system/drivers" pair is quite simple: let us take the example of the Word word-processor in the process of printing. Word announces to Windows: "I want to print". Windows receives the text and indicates to the printer, via the driver, that one of its applications wants to print. Windows translates the Word format to the format of the printer and sends the whole thing via the driver.

This set of system software programs which communicate with one another is essential for the correct operation of a PC. Nevertheless, they are not free from faults, which may greatly compromise the performance of a computer. It is for this reason that we will sometimes have to renew them using "updates". We will return to this essential in detail in Hours 6 and 7.

Versions, patches and updates
As time goes by, software programs improve and develop as a result of the continuous work of their designers. It is therefore possible to improve a PC's tools using updates. There are a number of types:

- *Patches are the simplest type of update: they are little pieces of software which correct minor faults in a product by modifying it slightly.*

- ***Updates*** *are more sizeable modifications of a product: they often force a complete installation. In the end, your product is visually identical, but several small faults may have been corrected.*

- ***Versions*** *are completely new software programs which replace the previous ones. They have increased functionality and sometimes the appearance or working of the software is altered. Windows 95 is a new version of the old Windows 3.1, for example.*

You will sometimes encounter the terms "Release, "Service Pack", or "Upgrades" which also describe product updates.

Bugs

A bug is a fault, error or omission in any software program from the simplest, which makes your computer run (the BIOS), to the operating system (Windows), including applications (Word, Excel, CorelDraw, etc.). The famous Pentium calculation fault which was in the news a few years ago was a bug in the software contained in the microprocessor.

A bug is therefore an error or fault produced by a faulty program under certain circumstances. It may turn up often (in poor software), occasionally, or even never (if you never use the faulty function, for example).

All the software programs in your PC, without exception, are completely overrun by bugs, but you will almost never encounter the majority of them: they lodge most often in functions which are rarely used, and which are therefore seldom checked.

Having said this, the newer the software, the more numerous and sometimes catastrophic are the bugs, as in the case of an old bug in Microsoft Word which erased text. It is common knowledge that the first versions of the Microsoft operating systems (Windows 95 1.0, MS-DOS 3.0, MS-DOS 6.0) are still full of bugs. Windows 95 is no exception to the rule and has yielded many bugs: these generally cause system instability in certain situations, and sometimes even cause the machine to stop.

To keep a PC in top condition, you must therefore periodically install driver or system updates which remove bugs. We will return to this aspect of PC maintenance in more detail in Hours 6 and 7.

Viruses

The whole world has heard of viruses. These are pieces of software whose purpose may be peaceful or offensive. They are introduced into your PC via a diskette or a downloaded software program into which they have been grafted.

You will see mention, in specialist literature, of "benign" and "malevolent" viruses. There are those which just establish themselves in the PC and display Hello for you in a corner of the screen, and others which, like the "Pacman crunchers", methodically devour the content of your hard disk.

Offensive or humorous, the virus is a piece of program which wanders about where it shouldn't and may cause serious disorder in your PC. They should be eradicated and every step taken to prevent their occurence. We will return to them in more detail in Hour 8.

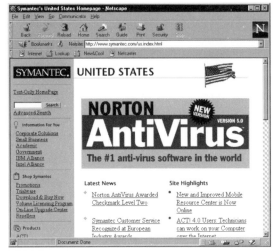

Figure 1.3: Viruses can be disastrous for PCs and must be eradicated using specialised utilities

Hour 2

Rules for good management

THE CONTENTS FOR THIS HOUR

- Normal shutdown
- What to do in the event of any problems
- Installing and storing software intelligently
- A clean and well-maintained PC
- Other memory
- Siting of the machine

The first step in keeping a PC in top condition is to get into the habit at the outset of carrying out a few simple actions.

Normal shutdown

A few years ago, you just needed to press the button when you wanted to turn off your PC. Today this is no longer possible. It is inadvisable, even dangerous, and for this reason Windows 95 contains in its Start menu a procedure called "Shut Down".

Each application of a PC, software or other, opens and closes files on the disk. As long as the file is not closed, the data it contains is not considered to be saved. The result is that if a PC is turned off without closing the files, this data is lost!

The disk cache
The disk cache is a software device which stores in a PC's central memory all the data recorded onto or read from the disk. This intelligent device starts from the assumption that an item of data is read or written 10 to 20 times more quickly using central memory than a hard disk. It will therefore always try to anticipate your requirements, attempting to foresee what you will want to read shortly from the hard disk, and preparing this data in memory. It is intelligent, and it works!

This apparently unnecessary process (you may raise the objection that once it is written on to the disk, the data should be there whatever happens) is in reality very practical. Your PC is equipped with a "cache" device which is used to speed up exchanges and to also increase the speed with which data is read or written. Consequently, this cache, which is a hardware assembly composed of memory, loses its content in the event of a loss of power. The Windows 95 Shut Down function therefore checks, before giving you clearance to turn off the machine, that all files are closed and the cache emptied.

You must always therefore turn off your computer using the procedure suggested by the software manufacturers. These steps are as follows:

1. Save the files created with your applications programs (spreadsheets, text files, etc.).

2. Close your applications programs.

3. Open the **Start** menu.

4. Click on **Shut Down**.

5. Wait until the black screen with the words "You may now shut down your computer" is displayed.

6. Switch off the computer.

In the event of a power failure
You may say that there are sometimes unforeseeable events against which nothing can be done: a power failure, for example.

In these cases, Windows 95 detects an abnormal shutdown and automatically runs the ScanDisk application when it is next started up. Reply yes to all the questions and it will automatically rectify any errors which this enforced shutdown may have caused.

Figure 2.1: The Shut Down function in the Start menu

Avoiding electrical problems

Some users are vulnerable to sudden changes in the mains electricity. In certain regions, for example, a small thunderstorm is a source of sudden voltage changes, not to mention "micro-disconnections". The latter, invisible to the naked eye, cause a short electrical stoppage. Although the majority of PCs tolerate them, data are still vulnerable. A micro-disconnection, without causing the machine to stop, may nevertheless generate a write error on the hard disk. This error (which will, for example, take the form of an erroneous character) may very well cause the total destruction of the file a few weeks later. If you use your PC under such conditions, you should buy an uninterruptible power supply. This will make the mains electricity completely reliable, acting as a substitute in the event of power failure.

WHAT TO DO IN THE EVENT OF ANY PROBLEMS

Obviously, whatever precautions are taken, the "zero fault" situation will not exist. You will, therefore, sometimes be confronted with a "locked up" application, perhaps even with the whole of the system being locked up. Here are a few rules to be followed in these cases:

- First, wait a few minutes. Do not attempt to resolve the problem by turning off the machine.

- Sometimes, a window will be displayed saying "This application is no longer responding": try, if applicable, to click on **End Task** to regain control. When it is displayed a second time, click on **Shut Down**.

- If the PC is locked up and nothing is happening, use the **Ctrl+Alt+Del** key combination, which will lead to the display of the **Close Program** window. Look in the list for the one followed by the **No Response** text, select it with the mouse and click on **Shut Down**.

- If the **Ctrl+Alt+Del** combination doesn't work, wait for five minutes and turn the PC off . The wait may allow the system to resolve the problem. On restart, Windows will run ScanDisk and clean up any faults.

Blue screens and error windows

Sometimes the error will take the form of a blue screen with bizarre wording, or a window indicating an "error in a module". In both these cases, Windows has detected an error about which it can do nothing, and it cannot indicate to you, in its own language, what has happened. In other words, its screens and windows are entirely unusable. There's nothing to be done but restart the PC.

Never carry on using an unstable PC

In all cases, when a PC system becomes "unstable", i.e. when an application starts to generate errors, or the whole systems fails, it is highly inadvisable to carry on using the PC. Even if the PC seems to have righted itself as a result of your operations, you should attempt to permanently stabilise the machine by shutting it down and then restarting it.

In the event of a problem, restart everything
Always restart your computer after an incident. Don't try to work on a PC whose system is unstable.

Figure 2.2: The Crash window following an error

The following is a specific example, from a reader's letter, of what may cause a PC to crash.

> *When I start Windows 95, the Desktop is displayed normally, but as soon as I click on an icon, or on a program in the **Start** menu, the error message "Explorer has caused a page fault in the "unknown" module at 0000:63634120" appears. I just need to click on **Close** and everything returns to normal. Is there a solution?*

Here is my reply: this phenomenon is abnormal and ... inexplicable! This sometimes occurs when some of the system files are corrupt (as a result of a power failure or a write error). If, as you told us, nothing has been modified in your configuration, the failure is probably due to a system write error or to the PC being shut down without going through the Windows Shut Down procedure. In any event, there is a single solution, also recommended by Microsoft technical support: reinstall Windows. Your old configuration will be saved, and your system will be updated.

Recovery tools

Some utility programs such as Nuts and Bolts or Norton (see the Appendix for a description of these products) offer functions for recovering from incidents. These tools are highly practical and considerably limit the risks of data destruction as a result of software crashes. Their specific task is to attempt to "recover" from an error and give you access to the faulty program. However, do not use these accessories indiscriminately. Although Nuts and Bolts recovers your software, this is not in order to make it possible for you to continue working as if nothing has happened, but to make it possible to save your work and then restart the system in order to stabilise it.

Figure 2.3: The Nuts and Bolts recovery window

Furthermore, when such tools are called upon too often, it means that your system is not in top condition, and that it's time to think about repairing it by reading the hours which follow.

INSTALLING AND STORING SOFTWARE INTELLIGENTLY

One good way to obtain an efficient PC is intelligent management of programs and their files: the more you scatter them about, the less organised you become.

- Consider installing all the programs in the directory intended for them: Program Files, situated in the Windows 95 root of the hard disk. This will make them easier to find again.

- Group your files together in subject folders: for example, all the text files in a "text" directory, if necessary divided into subdirectories.

- Avoid saving your files in the Windows Desktop, which, paradoxically, is often a source of muddle.

- Use long file names ("text on birds.doc" rather than "tobs.doc") which are quicker to identify when tidying up.

Keep a careful watch on everything concerned with storage: your disk must always have at least 10% free space available, and ideally 20%. Beyond this threshold, congestion occurs, performance drops and certain programs start to encounter problems. If your disk is congested, clean it (see Hour 3) or add a new disk. In the next hour, we will return to the problem of filing in detail.

Figure 2.4: Files and programs must be correctly stored away

 *To check the available capacity on a disk, click on **My Computer**, select the relevant disk, right-click with the mouse and select **Properties** from the drop-down menu. Click on the **General** tab to display the disk capacity.*

A CLEAN AND WELL-MAINTAINED PC

Maintenance of the PC and its "man/machine" interfaces is not just a means of having a better life with a clean PC. Dust, enemy number one of the computer, is unsightly, but also abrasive, and it destroys, erases, and makes things go wrong. A PC in top condition is therefore a clean PC. A good reason for devoting a few lines to cleaning the PC:

You should be aware that your PC attracts dust which clogs up everything, and, because it is abrasive, wears away, destroys, scratches and erases. You must regularly clean your screens, central unit covers and all the plastic fronts of the peripherals in order to prevent dust accumulating and creeping into the whole machine. These operations are particularly important if you smoke, since nicotine converts dust into a greasy film.

Dust is abrasive

Dust is abrasive: it is therefore capable, in theory, of scratching all the magnetic peripherals of a PC: the CD-ROM, floppy disk drives and the hard disks. Although these first two peripherals can be victims, your hard disk is theoretically not at risk. This is because it is factory-sealed and totally dust-proof. However, the dust may slowly destroy the electrical contacts and, in the long term, cause a disk failure.

Keyboard and mouse

In any event, there are at least two peripherals which you absolutely must maintain: the keyboard and the mouse. These peripherals, which are subject to mechanical actions, lose their efficiency, and perhaps even break down, under the effect of the accumulation of dirt. A key which no longer pushes in, or which produces two letters, is often the result of dust. The mouse which has to be rolled along two or three times to reach the targeted icon or menu can also be the result of dust.

For the keyboard, use an aerosol, which, through its blowing action, clears the accumulated dust. For the mouse, regularly dismantle the ball and clean the three rollers, which are used to transmit movements, with a moistened cotton bud. The ball must also be cleaned with a damp cloth and the dust removed from its housing with an aerosol. Special cotton buds for keyboard and mouse are sometimes sold with solutions ready for use. You just need to soak the cotton then clean the gaps. However, a cotton bud moistened with methylated spirits or surgical spirit gives the same result for much less cost.

The printer

As regards the printer, think about the print heads and cartridges. Inkjet cartridges and print heads, in particular, are equipped with their own intelligence and transmit their status to the printer. There are little copper tracks situated under the cartridge which you need to inspect. They quickly become covered with ink debris and may make the printer operation erratic. Clean them regularly with a cotton bud.

Protection

There are also many protective aids which reduce the need for maintenance: keyboard guards, screen covers, printer covers and so on. Some other protective products are less important, for example, anti-static foam whose function is to prevent dust being attracted by the computer. Admittedly, it limits the attraction of dust on the surface of the screen, but not inside, and still less on the central unit. Even with these foams, the equipment must still be cleaned regularly.

OTHER MEMORY

Also, from time to time, you should think about cleaning your floppy disk and CD-ROM drives with an aerosol (to blow the dust away). You will prevent risk of misalignment (loss of adjustment of read head accuracy) and dust being deposited on your diskettes or CD. You may wish to complete maintenance of the drive by using a cleaning diskette. If your CDs are covered with dust, use the damp cloths sold in shops, which prevent scratches.

With a clean PC, well-maintained peripherals and diskettes and CDs safe from the abrasive action of time, your PC will have a better and longer life, with no problems or incidents.

SITING OF THE MACHINE

A PC and its hard disks are sensitive to magnetic fields. These fields are liable to affect the data which they contain and so any source of magnetic field is therefore to be prohibited close to the PC. Thus the following should apply:

- television screens must be at least one metre away;

- cordless telephones must be at least one metre away;

- electrical equipment (drills, microwave ovens) must be at least one metre away; and

- GSM telephones must be at least two metres away for a 1 W model.

Hour 3

Tidying the hard disk

THE CONTENTS FOR THIS HOUR

- Reorganising your hard disk
- Old versions of software
- The Windows 95 Recycle Bin
- Cleaning the hard disk

A congested hard disk is a common phenomenon. Although the size of disks is constantly increasing (5 Mb with the first PCs, whereas now gigabytes are standard), the need of software programs is growing at the same time. Nevertheless, a number of users, by cluttering their PCs up with unnecessary files, using space thoughtlessly and not giving consideration to the organisation of their hard disk, do not realise how disorganised their disk is. Remedial action needs to be taken which will help you to save space, and even money. You may well not need a 1 Gb hard disk if your 500 Mb disk already contains 300 Mb of files which are no longer needed.

REORGANISING YOUR HARD DISK

Organising your hard disk is a matter of correct filing so that you are easily able to locate what is needed and remove what is no longer useful. If you have ten versions of compression programs (such as pkzip, lharc, Zip) in ten different places, 10 Mb of space is lost. Shareware programs and games from diskettes issued with magazines, ditto; not to mention identical drawings which are stored in five different directories corresponding to five applications programs capable of using them.

The first and most important step is therefore to reorganise your hard disk with a directory for each category of file. Let's take images as an example. Don't store them according to the format or applications program any more, but by subject. Don't use the **Draw** directory in Corel, the **Paint** directory in Photo Paint, and so on. Create an **Images** directory, with subdirectories Work, House, and Drawing and put all the image files in these, not making distinctions between formats. Already, you will note with amazement the number of redundant files. Proceed in the same way for the utilities, with a **Utilities** directory and **Compression Programs**, **Disk**, and **Multimedia** subdirectories, and yet more redundant files may be deleted. Better still, if you build complex applications, for example multimedia projects, don't store your data in the directories of the programs which edit them, but instead group them together by project.

OLD VERSIONS OF SOFTWARE

All software users are, sooner or later, confronted with the problem of versions. Whether you change from Corel 5 to Corel 6, from Toolbook 3 to Toolbook 4, from Word 4 to Word 95, the result is always the same; new software on the hard disk, and the old one kept "just in case". Only this "just in case" is 20 to 30 Mb lost with Corel and the same with Word. Microsoft Office takes up almost 100 Mb! The old version most frequently kept on your hard disks is Windows 3.1, kept when Windows 95 is installed. If you find the new version of software satisfactory, then remove the older version. Always reply "yes" when a software installation asks you to delete the old version. Otherwise, go to Hour 4 for a detailed explanation on the art of installing and uninstalling software.

THE WINDOWS 95 RECYCLE BIN

Another phase of the tidying process is emptying the Recycle Bin because all these deletion operations have filled it with dozens of files. They are deleted in effect, but not physically. It is therefore now a good idea to empty the Recycle Bin. Click its icon, open the **File** menu and select the **Empty Recycle Bin** option. Also consider deleting all the shortcuts, icons and icon groups which lead to programs you have deleted. Nothing is more annoying than to continually click on icons for non-existent programs or files.

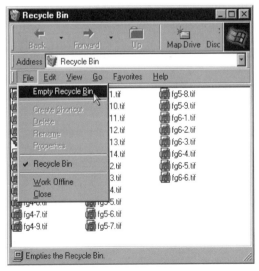

Figure 3.1: Emptying the Recycle Bin

▰▰▰ Directly deleting unnecessary files on the hard disk

Not all the files which have become obsolete are contained in the Recycle Bin. The hard disks contain a multitude of small files which are no longer needed. These include:

- copies of files made by the system (each time you save a text file, most editing tools and word processors make a copy "just in case");

- temporary files, created by programs for their operational requirements and deleted once their task is complete;

- your own files which are no longer useful; and

- numerous files installed by several programs and which no-one will ever use.

All these unnecessary files are easy to spot: they have particular extensions (the extension is the sequence of three letters which follows a dot after the name of a file: for example, .exe is an extension which signifies an executable program).

The files which occupy space needlessly generally have the following extensions:

- .bak: generally a replaced bat file;

- .pro: a replaced driver or program;

- .$$$: a very old file whose use is no longer remembered;

- .old: an old file; and

- .chk: a file of lost data generated by a disk scanning utility.

However, this list is not exhaustive! Abandoned Word files sometimes have the tilde sign (˜) at the beginning of their name. Files ending in ".---" are also encountered. Sometimes, it is a complete directory which is out of date: this ends with the extension ".$$$" or starts with " ˜ ".

These files can be deleted

- by using Windows Explorer; or

- by using an MS-DOS window.

The simplest solution is to use Windows Explorer. Open a disk's window. In **View**, select **Arrange Icons by Type** and look for files with the extensions mentioned above. Select them and either press the **Del** key to delete them or drag them to the Recycle Bin.

To delete unnecessary files in MS-DOS, open a window by clicking on the **Programs** option, then MS-DOS Commands, in the **Start** menu. From the "C:>" prompt, type, for example, "DIR *.BAK / S". In this example, all directory paths containing ".BAK" files will be displayed. You then access them by typing "cd \dirname" and delete them by entering the command "DEL *.BAK". Repeat this procedure for all extensions.

Lack of experience?

If you are not experienced, delete your unnecessary files by dragging them to the Recycle Bin. In the event of a mistake, you just need to drag them in the other direction, that is from the Recycle Bin to a disk window, in order to retrieve the file which was deleted in error.

Let's finish by mentioning files with the extension .tmp: some are contained in a directory ".tmp" in the root of the hard disk. These are temporary Windows files. As a general rule, these should be kept, except when they are isolated for no reason somewhere on the hard disk.

If you choose to destroy them, close all your applications beforehand: this will ensure that you don't destroy a file which is essential to a program during its operation.

Never delete swp files
You will sometimes encounter on your hard disk a very large file with the extension .swp (for example, win386.swp): never delete this as it is the Windows 95 "virtual memory" file, a device which makes it possible to compensate for a possible shortage of random access memory on your PC. Keep it as it is: Windows will delete it when it no longer requires it.

Enemy files

These are "naturally large" files consisting of images, "scanner" files or sound and video sequences.

An AVI video file frequently reaches around 100 Mb so you must be absolutely certain that you need it to justify keeping it! The "enemy" extensions to keep an eye out for are the following:

- .bmp: MS Paint image files;
- .avi: files containing video;
- .gif: image files which are not very large but which can quickly spread;
- .tif: very large image files, often associated with scanners;
- .pcl: files for printers which are very large and completely useless;
- .jpg: image files which are not very large but which can quickly spread; and
- .wav: large sound files, often installed with a sound card:

This list is not exhaustive, but if these types of file exist in your PC make sure that they are actually useful, and, if they are not, delete them! On all the PCs I have come across, this simple procedure usually saves more than 50 Mb! However little you defragment the disk after these operations (see below), your PC will probably increase its speed by 10 to 20%!

Deleting AVIs and BMPs from the Windows directory
Your Windows directory contains a number of files with
extensions .BMP and .AVI installed by the system for
decorating the Desktop. If you don't use them, delete them.
You will save several megabytes.

All the simple organisational operations that the user can perform
have now been described; it only remains for you to complete the
last phase on the hard disk: system cleaning.

CLEANING THE HARD DISK

Since the PC's system software programs are not fault-free, it often
happens that, during their work, they forget a few bits of "garbage"
or destroy a few items of data. They are there, somewhere on your
disk. You don't see them, but they clutter it up and, more serious,
may even one day seriously disrupt your programs. Windows 95
therefore offers two utilities for putting the finishing touches to
the disk tidying process: the Defragmenter and ScanDisk.

Use the utilities!
Faults which are apparently due to hardware are often in
fact due to software. This is the reason for the existence of
the Windows utilities Defragmenter and ScanDisk.

Defragmenting

Let's start with the Defragmenter. At best, a few users make use of
it once a month; at worst, never, yet it is an essential tool. It is used
to gather together all the files which have been distributed
throughout the hard disk, re-assembling them and arranging them
end to end. Why is this useful? The system, in managing the disk,
is constantly freeing up space and then filling it up again. If you
delete a 3 Mb file, a 3 Mb hole is left in the middle of the disk.
When the system next saves it fills this hole to economise on space.
However, it is probable that the next file to be recorded is not a 3

Mb file, but a file of 5, 10 or 20 Mb! The system therefore breaks
up the large file, placing sections of it into any spaces and adding
information in order to later re-assemble the scattered data.
Consequently, this slows things down, and consumes more space
than planned.

The fragmentation utility can lie...
*You have started the Windows defragmentation utility and
it gives you the message "4% — defragmentation not
required". Don't you believe it! 2% fragmentation is
sufficient to affect the performance of your PC. By way of
example, 4% of a 2 Gb disk is 81 Mb of mixed up files! So
defragment as often as possible, whatever the suggestions
of Windows 95 and Defragmenter.*

The Defragmenter, in re-assembling all these pieces and structuring
them, saves space but, above all – and this is the most important
thing – increases the performance of the disk by 10 to 50%. We
recommend that you defragment at least once a week, during your
lunch hour, for example. The operation takes a long time (several
hours) when it has never been carried out, but only takes a few
minutes when it is performed regularly. To access the Defragmenter
from Windows 95, use the **Start** menu, then **Programs**,
Accessories, and **System Tools** options.

Figure 3.2: The Defragmenter is sometimes an optimist!

Minimising the risks of fragmentation
The Windows 95 Virtual Disk file is always installed by default on the C: drive. Nevertheless, this location is not obligatory, and what is more, has a tendency to fragment your hard disk. Unfortunately, it is almost always on the C: drive that all the applications are installed. The solution is to create a small 200 Mb partition on an additional drive (a D: or an E: for example) and dedicate this partition to your virtual disk.

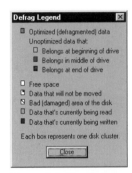

Figure 3.3: The Defragmenter reorganises the disk and gives it more vitality! Click on Legends to understand what the software screen is showing you

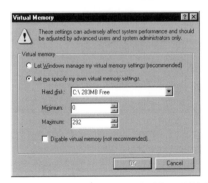

Figure 3.4: The Windows 95 Virtual Disk: a source of fragmentation

▬▬▬ Lost sectors and files: ScanDisk

ScanDisk is a tool complementary to the Defragmenter. Whilst the latter works on reorganising the disk and improving the arrangement of its content, ScanDisk itself works on the hard disk medium. Its function is to check and correct the physical structure of the disk. A power failure or software fault results in pieces of forgotten data on the hard disk. These pieces correspond to nothing, belong to no application, and yet they are there and occupy space. ScanDisk's first task is to find these pieces and eradicate them.

ScanDisk is also responsible for checking the organisation of directories and, if necessary, correcting structural errors or "crossed references".

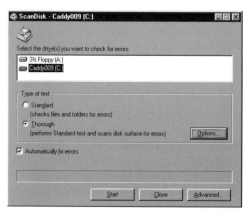

Figure 3.5: ScanDisk is the essential companion for your hard disk

A hard disk is organised into two main areas: one area contains the structure of the directories and the files which they contain and another contains the data corresponding to this directory. It is just like a diary: on one side the alphabetic tabs, on the other the names which correspond to the letter on the tab.

These two areas sometimes develop software or hardware faults, which affects the structure of the directories (for example, the files are no longer accessible normally and you get the message "file not found") and the content of the files (for example, an incomprehensible text is displayed). In these rare situations, it is necessary to analyse, repair and correct. This is what ScanDisk does. The main options of this program allow a "standard analysis" or a "thorough analysis". The analysis is used to check the content of the disk, and, if necessary, correct any errors found. The differences are:

- the standard analysis is limited to the file structure and to "gross" errors. The check is limited to a check of the file organisation; it does not check whether files are readable, or if part of the hard disk is damaged; and

- the thorough analysis, also called a "surface examination", carries out a structural check and a check of the functionality of the disk. In other words, it attempts to write and read each portion of the disk, and in this way checks that no area is unfit for use as a result of data destruction (possible reasons for data destruction will be discussed later).

With a standard analysis, you remove the garbage and the most common errors and this is quite often sufficient. You simply take the risk of correcting a fault without resolving its cause. If a portion of the disk is damaged, it will not be marked as unusable, and one day you risk writing some data to that place on the disk. However, newer disks are rarely subject to this type of fault.

Why are portions of disks destroyed?
The hard disk is composed of a magnetised material. It is on this medium that tracks are traced which then receive a format, and your data. The disk can fall prey to a localised magnetic fault capable of destroying one of its storage areas. This destroyed area is limited in size, but all the same it must be indicated to the software since it is not usable and causes read and write errors.

How to use ScanDisk

To access the ScanDisk utility, open the **Start** menu, then select **Programs**, **Accessories**, **System Tools**. Click on the **ScanDisk** icon to start it.

You can select the standard or the thorough option. In practice, it's a good idea to run a standard analysis frequently (each week) and a thorough analysis at least once a month or following a standard analysis which has failed.

You can configure a number of ScanDisk options by clicking on **Advanced**. The default configuration offered to you is fine and you can make do with it. If you are a perfectionist, tick the **Free** box under lost file fragments: all the pieces of lost files encountered will automatically be destroyed. Otherwise, they will be converted into files with the extension "chk" which you can delete later.

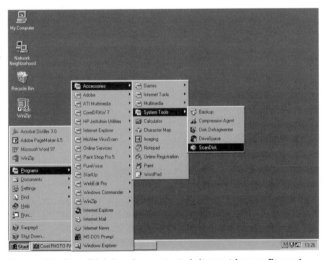

Figure 3.6: ScanDisk has been started; it must be configured

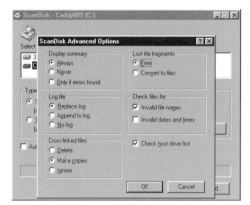

Figure 3.7: Configuring the software

Start with a standard analysis by clicking on the **Standard** tick-box, then on **Start**. ScanDisk analyses the disk and, if necessary, corrects any errors. Repeat the operation for each hard disk in your PC.

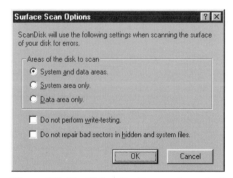

Figure 3.8: Modifying the thorough analysis options

When you have some free time, try running a "thorough" analysis. Be careful, this operation may take several minutes and it is inadvisable to interrupt it.

In this mode, by clicking on **Options**, you can select the area of the disk to be analysed: the directory structure area, the data area, or both. Select both by ticking the **System and data area** option. However, tick the box **Do not repair bad sectors in hidden and system files**. In the event of errors encountered in this area, this operation could lock up your PC; it would therefore be as well, in this particular case, to keep the errors temporarily as they are.

About CHKDSK

Your Windows 95 system also provides you with a disk check utility called CHKDSK. You can try typing this command in a DOS window. However, this software is a relic from the old versions of MS-DOS and Windows, and is much less efficient and user-friendly than ScanDisk.

Room to express yourself

Your hard disk is now perfectly healthy, but this is temporary. These cleaning and restructuring operations must be run periodically to ensure their effectiveness. The more often you clean up your hard disk, the shorter the operation will be. There are other benefits: since programs are not always designed to deal with extreme situations, including congestion and disorganisation of a disk, a disk which is well ordered and cleaned will limit the risk of a fault in your PC's system.

Hour 4

Installation procedures

THE CONTENTS FOR THIS HOUR

- Installation
- Correct installation
- What to do when things go wrong

The installation and uninstallation processes on a PC are important activities. In this hour, we shall study the installation of both applications software and drivers. The installation of a system (for example, Windows 98), where a more complex mechanism is involved, will be dealt with in the second part (Hour 12). We shall look at uninstallation in Hour 5.

INSTALLATION

Installation involves transferring software or an upgrade to your PC and making it operational. It also involves installing programs and peripheral drivers.

What is installation?

As we saw in Hour 1, the PC is an assembly of various peripherals and items of hardware, put together to achieve compatibility. It is therefore necessary to prepare software not only to recognise your configuration but also to meet your requirements.

Software, as delivered on CD-ROM or diskettes, is not immediately operational. You have to install it using your computer's installation program. There are various kinds of installation:

- **The installation of "major software programs"**: a word processor, or a database, with particular features for each one.

- **The installation of utilities**: simple tools for making daily life easier. Nuts and Bolts or antivirus software are examples of these utilities.

- **The installation of hardware drivers**: interfaces which manage peripherals such as a scanner or a printer.

- **The installation of system drivers**: little pieces of software which add a function to the system.

There are therefore a number of types of installation (there are four categories here, but you may encounter others), but, for each one, there are small differences which you need to know to keep your computer in good condition. Here is more information on each category.

The major software program

Most software programs are very large. Besides the application itself, the CD-ROM for this product contains a multitude of additional files. Fonts, sometimes images, help files, additional modules (the WordArt utility for Word, for example, or the equation editor for Excel), as well as hardware drivers, utilities and system drivers.

Utilities

In general, utilities are easily installed. However, they are potentially capable of causing major problems and modifications to your system. Antivirus software, for example, is installed so that it runs automatically when the machine is started up. It is therefore always there and may interfere with the operation of other applications. This is what is referred to as background operation. You have to be careful when installing a utility, as it may replace another accessory already existing in the system, such as ScanDisk or Defragmenter, for example.

Figure 4.1: Installing a major software program is the most sophisticated but also the most complex installation procedure. This figure shows the content of the Office CD-ROM and its installation procedures

The peripheral driver

A peripheral driver is either detected and installed by the system, or contained on a diskette, in which case it is necessary to run the start-up program. When it is detected by the system, the driver is most often simply added. You may have to configure it, but that isn't the subject for this hour. On the other hand, the driver installed from a diskette's **Install** or **Setup** program is sometimes more problematic. The installation programs for a sound card, for example, often add utilities to the hard disk, and maybe even sound files, which occupy space and are seldom used. They sometimes replace the Windows Multimedia Drive with a tool which takes up more space and machine power. The same applies to scanner drivers associated with drawing tools which are not used – more of these later.

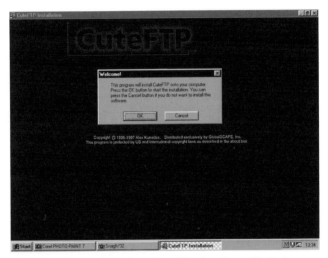

Figure 4.2: The installation of a utility is a formality but can include pitfalls

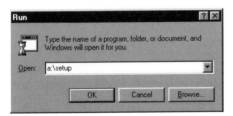

Figure 4.3: Peripherals are quick to install: just run Install or Setup

The system driver

Let us finish with the system driver. You can use this to add a new video format, for example, or Internet functions. It is often easy to install and occupies little space. ActiveX, Indeo and Quicktime, which enable the PC to recognise new types of video format, are system drivers. They help keep your computer in good condition, because some of them are capable of using advanced PC functions, such as working in 32-bit or 16-bit mode. They can also be used to reserve resources such as memory in order to maximise operating efficiency. Used correctly, system drivers help you get the most out of your PC.

Installing patches
Patches are pieces of software which modify another program in order to correct its errors. The installation of a patch is therefore the execution of a modification program. Patches are self-explanatory except that they sometimes generate .PRO or .BAK files, which you should delete.

Installation risks

Before going any further, it is worth spending a few minutes of this hour on installation risks, since it is very often from the installation process that the majority of problems and malfunctions which you may encounter arise. An incorrectly followed installation procedure may harm the efficiency of your PC by:

• proliferating unnecessary files;

• replacing programs without preparation;

• automatically starting unnecessary applications or utilities; or

• muddling up register bases and initialization and system files.

What is a register base and a system file?
You will often hear terms such as "register base", "system file" or "initialization files" when using your PC. These

are files containing information enabling Windows 95 to operate. Register bases, for example, contain the references and options for all your software programs and your system. These include screen colours, character fonts, directories containing data, etc. Initialization files (terminated with .INI) do the same thing, but are relics of the old versions of Windows (2.0, 3.X). All these files must be up to date and contain no errors for your computer to operate properly.

If you do encounter a problem, don't worry. It's more likely to be a fault with the computer software and its installation tools than something you've done yourself.

CORRECT INSTALLATION

Many of the Install or Setup programs on your diskette or CD-ROM are quite sophisticated, so the first thing to do is learn how to run the installation program properly.

Ideal installation

The first choice offered by an installation program is often between:

- default installation;

- customised installation;

- maximum installation; and

- minimum installation.

With utilities, the choices will sometimes be limited.

Understanding these options is not very complicated. The content of most CD-ROMs or diskettes is enormous, and is designed to cope with not only all existing PC types but also your own personal requirements, which may not be the same as your neighbour's.

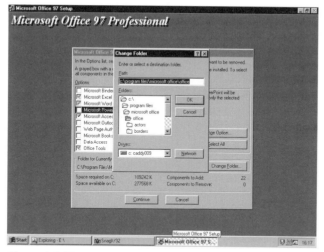

Figure 4.4: The installation procedure for MS Office offers many choices of directory

These options are summarised below:

- default installation is suitable for everyone. Remember that it is general purpose, and therefore not necessarily adapted to your own wishes;

- customised installation allows you to select your own options, modules, and tools, i.e. to manage the way in which the software will be installed on your PC. We shall describe this in more detail later;

- maximum installation transfers everything which is on the CD to your PC, clogging up the hard drive with useless data and making software programs unnecessarily complex;

- minimum installation can be a good, economical solution, but may not install all the tools you require, and is therefore not recommended; and

- the choice of directory allows you to install the software where you want it on your hard disk, rather than have dozens of applications scattered randomly across your system.

The default path

The default location describes where your programs will be stored on your hard disk. As a general rule, the programs will be installed by default in the root of the hard disk (C:\Program_name\). However it is better, especially if you only have one hard disk, to store your applications in the directory C:\Program Files. To do so, proceed as follows:

1. Using the **Explore** button, select **C:\Program Files**.

2. If the first thing you get contains a folder name, for example, C:\MS_Office\MSWORD\, add, after the path C:\Program Files, the name of the program directory, that is C:\Program Files\MSWORD\.

3. The installation tool will take care of the rest.

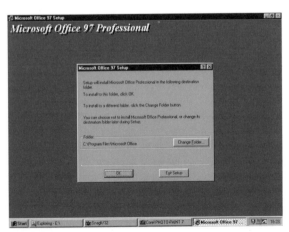

Figure 4.5: The choice of default path

If you have more than one hard disk

If you have more than one hard disk, or one disk divided into several partitions (accessible by means of several letters), store all your programs on the disk which is fastest and has the most free space. But be careful: a 500 Mb disk which already contains Windows might well become congested more quickly. Therefore, with this type of configuration, avoid installing your tools and programs on the same disk as the system. Permanent congestion would risk making it unstable.

Choosing the bit mode

Some programs may ask you to select a bit mode before you do anything else. You will have a choice of two options:

- install in 16-bit mode; or

- install in 32-bit mode.

The simple rule is this: if your PC works with Windows 95 and, at the very least, a Pentium, choose the 32-bit mode.

The mode corresponds to the method used by the software to communicate with the processor. In other words, the more bits there are, the more quickly this will happen: communicating in 32 bits makes it possible to exchange twice as much information as in 16-bit mode in the same unit of time, that is, one processor cycle.

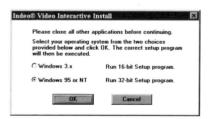

Figure 4.6: Don't select the 16-bit or 32-bit modes without proper consideration

You will come across this question with installation procedures for peripheral drivers (for CD-ROM drives or graphics cards), for certain software programs (graphics programs in particular) and system drivers (especially for video display).

Anyway, it's probable that when you open this book in 2001, the software will offer you a 64-bit mode (some installation procedures for graphics card drivers do so already). We recommend you check in the system documentation that the system is compatible with the desired mode, and select the most efficient bit mode.

Using the Customized Installation option

The **Customized Installation** option, offered when a software program is large, makes it possible to choose precisely all the components of the software to be installed on the hard disk. To select it, just click on its button.

Once in this mode, the installation software will display a list of its components: you just need to tick or untick the boxes to agree to the installation or not. In the best installation procedures, especially those of Microsoft, Lotus or Corel, the space which the software will occupy on the hard disk will be updated automatically along with your selections.

Here are a few tips for best installation.

Avoid unnecessary fonts

Character fonts may each take up 120 Kb on your hard disk: therefore don't install them with your software as a matter of course. Read the manual, look at the appearance of the font, and select the one or ones which suit you. In Windows, all fonts are compatible with one another: those already installed will also work in your new software. Therefore it's unnecessary, in many cases, to add more.

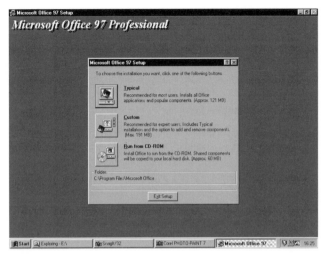

Figure 4.7: Use the Customized Installation option if possible

Don't download too many fonts
Too many fonts sometimes impair the overall performance
of the machine. In the first versions of Windows 95, more
than 255 fonts even caused software and system crashes!
Very few users require more than around 50 fonts.
Therefore try to remain below this limit; never exceed 100
fonts.

You can also delete fonts at any time. Just open the **Control Panel**,
click on **Fonts** and right-click on the icon of the font to be deleted,
then select **Remove**.

Check by looking
To check that a font meets your requirements by looking at
*it, open the **Control Panel**, select the **Fonts** option and*
double-click on the name of the font you wish to check. A
page of text is then displayed using the font in question.

Avoid unnecessary programs

You don't necessarily need all the utilities delivered with your applications or installation diskette. Any tools, accessories and modules you don't want should therefore be removed. For example, get rid of WordArt if you only use your PC for typing text.

Avoid unnecessary files

Clipart (a databank of images), templates, on-line help, educational software: do you really need all the accessories supplied with your software? If not, remove them from your installation.

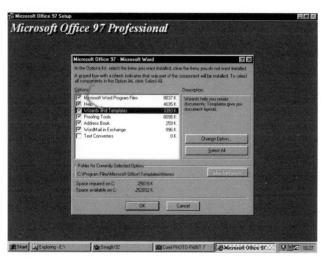

Figure 4.8: Avoid clipart and other files if you don't need them

▬▬▬ Using the Installation Wizard

The Installation Wizard is a set of windows specially designed by the configuration software to make life simpler for you. Its aim is to advise you when the installation program is preparing to modify your system. These windows are displayed at regular intervals during the process of installing the software and sometimes offer to change or modify files for you. They will also offer to:

- replace old files;
- replace drivers; and
- delete an old version of the software.

File replacements

An installation program will sometimes ask you to reply to the question "file x is newer than the one installed in your computer; do you want to keep this file or replace it?". The file in question is probably a driver, a utility or a set of tools. Since the newest version is bound to be more efficient, you should install it.

Why the correct date and time should be set on your PC
To manage the replacement of old versions of drivers and programs, installation programs always use the date and time of manufacture. Generally, this is assigned by the installation program, and not by your PC. However, the assignment of dates to files automatically made by the system is a good means of keeping a check on versions: it is a good idea therefore to always make sure that your clock has the correct date and time.

Replacing or adding system drivers

If you like games, you have probably noticed recently that, when you install a Microsoft product, the program offers to update "DirectX" to "DirectX 5.0". This set of system drivers, components of Windows, has the advantage of multiplying the display speed by a factor of two or three; yet another update with little expense which is carried out by means of an installation program. As a general rule, accept all suggestions for installation of system components: updates of drivers for CD-ROMs (MSCDEX), video (Active X, Direct X, Indeo, Quicktime), libraries (files with extension DLL), etc.

Replacing one application with another

The final question you will be asked by the installation software is whether you want to replace the old application with a new one. Always answer yes! It is pointless keeping several megabytes of data on your hard disk for a program which will no longer be used. Anyway, the installation programs always keep your old documents, so there is no danger of you losing them. Only the program is erased.

WHAT TO DO WHEN THINGS GO WRONG

You now have a list of procedures to follow based on the assumption that everything goes well. However, you should also be aware of what to do when things go wrong. Poor installation results in system file problems, unused disk space and poor computer operation.

The installation procedure can also abort, for a multitude of reasons:

- a peripheral in the PC is missing;

- a driver is missing;

- a first software program necessary for installing a second one is missing;

- there is insufficient space on the disk;

- the software publisher made a mistake; or

- the system is unstable.

Before examining the consequences and the actions to be taken as a result of an installation which has failed, here are a few words of advice for trying to sort it out:

- Check that all the peripherals are correctly configured and working (scanners, writers and modems). If, for example, you try to install a games software program that requires a joystick, installation will fail if the joystick is not configured correctly.

- Sometimes, it's the space available on the hard disk which runs out. With some tools, installation stops before the files are copied, but sometimes it stops during the copying and leaves a mass of unwanted data. Always try to make space on the disk before installing.

- A system error message (register base, faults in the module and so on) is a symptom of instability. Try turning off the computer, restarting it, and installing again.

- When nothing works, try phoning the software publisher. It is not uncommon for the installation procedure of software sold in the shops to be deficient. Very often, a little nudge in the right direction from the company's technical support department is enough to sort out the problem.

In any event, never immediately try to delete manually (with the Recycle Bin, for example) the files left by a failed installation. Always try to sort out the problem before reinstalling.

Quite often, this is sufficient. Sometimes, also, the installation progresses normally, but it is afterwards that things go wrong! File errors and other kinds of message are then displayed. Yet again, you need to try to understand the fault, remove it, and if necessary reinstall. Here are a few tips:

- "Sharing violation" messages mean that the installation program is trying to replace a file on the disk already being used by another application or by the system. Deactivate all the tools in the Taskbar (by clicking on them and selecting **End Task**) and close all active programs. Antivirus software is very often responsible for this type of message.

- "Runtime Errors" (execution errors), missing files and other "VBRUN absent" errors are almost always due to an installation program deficiency. In other words, the program works, but falls down on a particular characteristic of your PC. Refer to the documentation on the CD-ROM or diskette, called "readme.txt", or some other similar title. It will generally indicate the procedure to be followed for sorting out the problem, if necessary by adding a file to the system. Shareware programs and multimedia software (encyclopaedias, for example) are very often subject to this type of error.

Runtimes

Software designers sometimes use "development tools" for designing their applications. These are programs which are used to create other programs. The problem is the program created by another program needs the latter to work. As it is not permitted to supply a program which one does not own to accompany a program which one has created, software publishers supply a "Runtime". This is a piece of the development tool which is used only to make its applications work. The Runtime is essential to make certain software developed in this way work. Incorrectly installed, it can be a source of many errors.

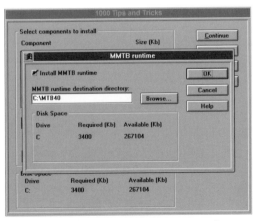

Figure 4.9: Runtimes are often a source of errors

The consequences of a failed installation

When an installation procedure aborts, it clutters up the hard disk and causes system changes. The next hour explains how to get rid of this unwanted data.

Reinstalling software

Software which starts to work incorrectly can very often be repaired by reinstalling it. This restores all the old modules of a program, and, consequently, those which are faulty, while keeping your data (text files, images, spreadsheets, etc.) safe.

Hour 5

Saving space and uninstalling

THE CONTENTS FOR THIS HOUR

- Uninstallation
- Applications programs, utilities and saving space

Now that you have learned how to install a program, you must learn how to uninstall it for when it is no longer of any use. If you don't, you will soon clutter up your hard disk to the point where it becomes unmanageable.

This hour deals with how to uninstall a program and with how to save space using a few interim solutions.

UNINSTALLATION

Uninstallation is as important as installation. A program which is no longer of any use occupies space needlessly, clutters up the system, and may cause problems in future. Observe the following guidelines to avoid overburdening your computer:

- don't collect software programs from diskettes supplied with magazines if you are never likely to use them;

- don't keep tools which you never use;

- don't keep twelve successive versions of the same software, unless you have an excellent reason; and

- don't keep the remnants from an aborted installation attempt.

With the advent of Windows 95, the problem of uninstallation has finally been taken into consideration, and is covered by a number of very efficient options:

- **Uninstallation by the system**: Windows 95 takes care of automatically deleting and cleaning up an application. This works well most of the time, but not always.

- **Uninstallation by the application**: an uninstallation tool is associated with a program, and you just need to run it to delete the program. This nearly always succeeds, and often better than the Windows 98 procedure.

- **Specialised uninstallation software**: an intelligent concept, but tricky to implement. We shall look at this later.

Uninstallation and register bases
In Windows 98, software which is installed adds "codes" to the register bases, the Windows 95 "system" files (see Hour 4).

> *When they remain despite an uninstallation, these codes clutter up the system unnecessarily and may impair its operation. It is therefore necessary to try to use the best installation procedure available to make sure that the codes of a software package will be deleted from a register base at the same time as its programs.*

These three solutions are fine when they work. However, we shall see that it is sometimes necessary to call up procedures that function quicker when none of these works (which does happen). Uninstall therefore, in this order of preference, using the following methods:

- the uninstallation tool delivered with the software;
- the Windows uninstallation functions.

When neither of the two work, use a specialised utility. If none of the preceding solutions work, uninstall manually.

Why this precise order? Why not, as a matter of course, use the standard Windows uninstallation capabilities? The reason is that the Windows uninstallation doesn't delete all the drivers or pieces of software belonging to an application, and therefore a solution which lacks performance and which leaves unwanted data. On the other hand, the uninstallation procedure associated with an applications program is much more exhaustive. It is specially designed for it and therefore more precise, and should always be your first choice.

Specialised utilities are very efficient and delete everything, but don't always work, which is why you shouldn't make them your first choice. Uninstallation programs, although very efficient, are like antivirus software programs. They have to follow technical developments and take into account the special features of certain programs, which takes a certain amount of time. The latest versions of uninstallation programs offer good solutions to problems, but are to be used only when nothing else works, for trying to sort out an uninstallation problem, for example.

Figure 5.1: Always use the uninstallation utilities delivered with the software if possible

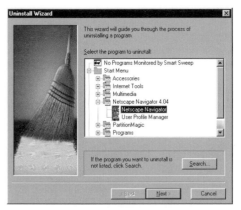

Figure 5.2: The specialised uninstallation programs are not always the most suitable

Uninstallation procedures in practice

We have seen the range of options but how do we actually go about uninstalling? The best procedure, the one delivered with a piece of software, is also the simplest to use. It is a program which can take several types of name. Here are a few examples:

- Corel Uninstaller uninstalls a program produced by the Corel company;

- Uninstall Cute FTP deletes a Cute FTP utility;

- Adobe software uses the phrase "Uninstallation of" followed by the name of the software program;

- Uninstall Xtramail deletes the Xtramail electronic mail software; and

- with certain applications the installation program takes care of uninstallation. This is the situation with the majority of Microsoft programs: with Office 97, you run **Installation** and click on **Add/Remove** to uninstall.

Here, a few examples have been given of the main uninstallation procedures you will encounter. Where do you find them?

In general, the uninstallation procedure accompanies the program: it is therefore displayed below its name, in the area dedicated to it, in the **Start** menu.

In other cases, this procedure is sometimes present, although without being displayed in the **Start** menu. In these cases, you have to go into **My Computer** and explore the application's CD-ROM in order to find it. Most often this takes the form of an icon in the shape of a computer with a blue screen. It may also be present on the hard disk: go into your program's directory using **Windows Explorer**, and look for it (hence the importance of having grouped your programs together in the **Program Files** directory).

Then uninstalling is easy: start the program, answer the questions, and everything should disappear.

Figure 5.3: The uninstallation procedure often accompanies the program

To make sure of this, explore the **Start** menu and check that the folder corresponding to the uninstalled program has disappeared. If this is not the case, right-click on the Taskbar, select **Properties**, then the **Programs** tab from the **Start** menu and finally **Delete**: delete the directory which is no longer of any use.

 Also check on your hard disk that nothing remains of the uninstalled program by exploring its directory. Delete what remains manually if necessary, by dragging the icons to the Recycle Bin.

 What remains after uninstallation is sometimes important. When an uninstallation program leaves a few directories and files on the hard disk, it is often because it has come across documents which belong to you! Before deleting everything manually to finish the uninstallation, check that you aren't going to destroy your own documents!

▬▬▬ The standard Windows procedure and the specialised utilities

If your program is not supplied with any uninstallation procedure, you may need to use the standard Windows procedure. Open the **Control Panel** and select the **Add/Remove Programs** icon. In the **Install/Uninstall** tab, a list of applications is displayed.

Figure 5.4: Windows now includes an uninstallation function

Scroll the list to the name of the program to be deleted, click on **Add/Remove**, reply Yes to the request for confirmation which follows, and let the system get on with it.

If, in the last window displayed, you see the following message at the bottom: "the uninstallation is complete, but it has not been possible to remove some items", you must finish the uninstallation manually:

- right-click on the Taskbar, select **Properties**, then the **Programs** tab from the **Start** menu and finally **Delete**. Check if the directory for the application has disappeared, and, if necessary, delete it; or

- check on your hard disk that nothing remains of the uninstalled program by exploring its directory. Delete what remains manually if necessary, by dragging the icons to the Recycle Bin.

Using a specialised utility program, the uninstallation procedure is similar to that of Windows.

When nothing works

If you've tried everything (the procedures provided by the software, those provided by Windows and those provided by a specialised tool) and still nothing works, you will have to remove everything manually, by deleting the directories. It is the only valid solution, but it risks causing significant problems in the operation of the system, and leaving a lot of unwanted data. Here are a few situations:

- the uninstallation procedure halts on an error;

- an installation procedure doesn't finish, and what remains cannot be uninstalled; or

- the uninstallation procedure doesn't exist.

In these three cases, it is likely that your system is destabilised. The best solution is to reinstall Windows in order to stabilise it (see Hour 12). It is also possible that your version of Windows is old and requires to be updated. In this case, refer to Hour 7.

However, before coming to that, you can try manual deletion. The procedure is identical to that already described in the preceding sections:

- Right-click on the Taskbar, select **Properties**, then the **Programs** tab from the **Start** menu and finally **Delete**; select the application's directory and delete it;

- then delete the program on the hard disk; select the icon for the application's directory by exploring your hard disk from My Computer, and drag it to the Recycle Bin.

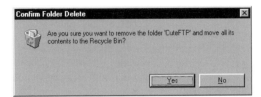

Figure 5.5: When nothing else works, the only thing that remains is manual uninstallation

Some remnants will probably remain. Here is a typical example:

> *I installed the Avast 32 antivirus software which I want to uninstall. Unfortunately, this operation seems impossible, since the utility is also activated as a background task as soon as Windows 95 starts. I therefore deleted its directory. The problem I have is that, when Windows starts up each time, I always get messages informing me that two shortcuts are missing: RGW.EXE and FGW.EXE. Could you tell me how to stop this message appearing during start-up?*

The messages "Missing Shortcuts" or "Link Absent" are typical symptoms of incorrect uninstallation. Here are a few general proposals for coping with this situation:

- Check that the files started automatically are not described in the [windows] section ("run" or "load" option) of the file win.ini. To edit this file, use the **Wordpad** tool from the **Start** menu, **Programs**, **Accessories** and open the file win.ini in the Windows directory. If applicable, delete the lines corresponding to the name of the missing program (in this example, RGW.EXE). However, this solution is not necessarily the only one – nor indeed the best.

- Check that the files in question are not present in the **StartUp** directory of the Windows **Start** menu (**Programs** option). This particular example was resolved by e-mail: the executable files were located in the **Start** menu.

Subsequent problems

These operations are to be carried out with great caution. If, afterwards, you experience many recurring errors such as "error in module", or "register base error", it is probably because your system is unstable as a result of an uninstallation problem. You should consider reinstalling Windows. Otherwise, continue working, but be careful!

APPLICATIONS PROGRAMS, UTILITIES AND SAVING SPACE

You don't need to uninstall every program your computer contains in order to keep it working properly. If you manage your programs properly, you will save space and work more efficiently.

▬▬▬ Using the Internet to explore and Outlook to delete

Internet tools are particularly greedy in terms of disk space. They spend their time archiving, storing and organising, and end up occupying large amounts of space, which can cause fragmentation of the disk and a loss of performance.

Electronic mail software

Electronic mail software stores all your messages. If you make your address public to all-comers, in books and magazines, or if, like the publisher of this book, you spend hours writing to your authors asking them for their manuscripts, and consequently receive dozens of replies every day, you quickly end up with a pile of correspondence. Fortunately, all electronic mail software packages allow you to compress your messages if they become too numerous. When your electronic mail software starts up, it will offer you the chance to compress your messages. In order to save space, always reply Yes.

Figure 5.6: Always answer Yes when an application offers to reorganise your files

Additionally, you should be aware that messages with attachments (images, texts) are all stored by your software: consider deleting them as soon as you don't need them any more. One hundred messages containing images with a size of 1 Mb needlessly use up 100 Mb of space. And in the case of messages with attachments, compression has almost no effect.

Don't forget either to select the message deletion option if you regularly use certain Newsgroups. These contain dozens of images, which also take up a lot of space. With Outlook, select the option **Tools**, **Options**, **Advanced**, and tick the boxes **Delete Messages**, and **Don't keep messages after reading**.

Browsers

Browsers (sometimes also called *Navigators*) keep track of all the pages you explore in their cache folder. Fortunately, this cache is configurable! After ten days of intensive surfing, the cache may easily exceed 100 Mb.

To set the cache with Microsoft Explorer, right-click on the
Explorer icon, and select **Properties**. Select the **General** tab and
click on **Temporary Internet File Settings**. Using the cursor,
select the maximum disk size you want to reserve for the Explorer
cache.

To avoid fragmenting the disk, while keeping a good quality of
Internet access (since the cache improves the page display speed),
associate a proxy server with a cache of around 20 Mb of data.

The proxy server is a computer belonging to the operator,
responsible for keeping in its memory all the pages requested
most often by user.

With this solution, the Internet operator's computers provide you
with your cache memory, thus freeing up your hard disk. To
configure the **Proxy** option, select the **Connection** tab and tick the
Connect to Proxy Server box.

The name of the proxy server will be provided by your operator.

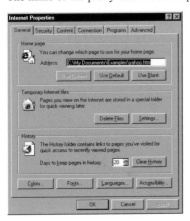

*Figure 5.7: Internet explorers are greedy on memory, so you
might want to consider adjusting their cache*

Saving images

If you are a keen user of graphics software, beware of certain image formats: some take up more memory than others. The BMP format, for example, of MS Paint, is not compressed, and therefore occupies ten to twenty times more space on a hard disk than a file in GIF format, for an identical image!

Always check, before saving your images, that there is no **Compression** option in the **Options** menu of the **Save** window. If there is, select it.

Disk doublers

We shall close this hour with disk doublers. These devices (badly named), do not actually double the size of the disk, but instead they compress all saved files.

The consequence of this is that a disk doubler has no effect on files which are already compressed, such as image, sound, or sometimes text files, whose saving method already provides compression. GIF, JPEG, AVI and MPEG files cannot be compressed, but databases often are, while executable programs sometimes are. If you work a lot with Internet HTML pages, images, and multimedia, compression will not work with these formats. On the other hand, for users of text, electronic office software, digital images, or vector drawings (produced with Corel Draw, Microsoft Publisher, or Autocad, for example), the disk doubler will probably give you a space saving of the order of 20 to 50%.

Windows 95 comes as standard with a compression tool called "Drive Space", accessible by selecting **Programs**, **Accessories**, **System Tools** from the **Start** menu. There are also others in the shops (Disk Doubler, for example).

A few important points to be aware of before rushing into the installation of these devices:

- Drive Space was a prime cause of MS-DOS 6.x disk malfunctions;

- Defragmenter doesn't work with a disk doubler;

- in the event of corruption of part of the "doubled" disk, all your data are lost; and

- a 2 Gb hard disk isn't really very expensive.

These tips are important to remember, so that you do not end up spending a great deal of time saving very little space. There is also the risk that your computer will malfunction.

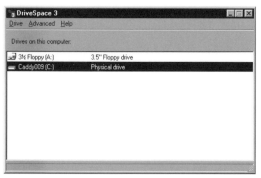

Figure 5.8: Disk doublers should be used with caution

Hour 6

Drivers

THE CONTENTS FOR THIS HOUR

- Introduction to drivers
- How to install a driver
- Versions and retrieval
- Windows 95 multimedia drivers
- Print drivers
- The future of drivers

Drivers are pieces of software responsible for controlling your computer's peripherals. Out of date drivers can cause malfunctions such as printing or screen problems. It is therefore important to keep your drivers up to date.

INTRODUCTION TO DRIVERS

When you encounter a peripheral problem, always start by asking yourself the following question: have I got the correct version of driver? To answer this question, you first have to understand what the driver actually does. Quite simply, the driver is used to make a peripheral (modem, screen, graphics card, etc.) understand what the system (Windows or DOS) and the software expect of it. But why does the system ask a third party – the driver – to do what it could do itself? The answer has to do with standards – or the lack of them.

Drivers and standards

The driver, a small software interface, has become necessary with the development of the PC. On old Apple computers, there were no drivers: a printer was an Apple printer and a screen was designed by Apple. In short, everything was standardised. However, with the PC only the Intel processor is standardised. Everything else can be designed, offered and sold by anyone who wants to do so.

This is where drivers come in, because, without standards, the system is not in a position to communicate with an interface without a suitable driver. It may be said therefore that it is the driver which has made the PC; it can also be argued that drivers are the number one cause of our computers' operating problems! They are all different and all have their little secrets. Let's take the example of a modem. Schematically, on a PC, the communication software requests **Telephone**, and the driver serves as the interface. It knows that, when it receives the command **Telephone** from the software, it must activate command x on a type x modem or y on a type y modem. In practice, as we shall see, this operation tends to be simplified.

How drivers modernised the PC

Thanks to the standardisation of equipment, drivers have enabled massive advances to be made in the computer world. Let's take the mouse as an example. Whether you use a Microsoft, Hewlett Packard or Logitech model, or one without a brand name, the standard Windows mouse driver works. This seems obvious, but, even ten years ago, imagine that each mouse was accompanied by its own diskette! The same applied to floppy disk drives as well, which, today, are managed directly by the PC BIOS, that is, at a level even lower than that of the Windows system even though, when the 3½" diskette format appeared, all the drives were managed by drivers, which meant that if you didn't have a driver, you couldn't insert any diskettes.

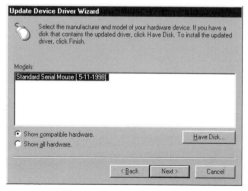

Figure 6.1: The oldest peripherals (e.g. the mouse) are most standardised

The system and the drivers

The advent of Windows 95 has removed a good number of driver problems, as Windows 95 automatically recognises almost all VGA graphics cards and modems and a good number of printers. This is known as Plug and Play.

Plug and Play
*This means you can put the expansion card in your
computer, which recognises it, and it does all the rest.*

Because the arrival of new standards, such as the SCSI hard disk format,
always disrupts the existing situation, you would need a driver to
operate a hard disk that complies with that format. The same applies
to 56,000 baud modems. Since these represent recent technology, they
are not recognised by Windows 95, in which case a driver is again
necessary. Generally, all multimedia peripherals, which are still poorly
standardised (with the exception of sound cards), need their own driver.
This is the case for video acquisition cards, CD-ROM writers, scanners,
and improved graphics cards, such as the Matrox models.

Figure 6.2: All peripherals need a driver

How to install a driver

For all recent generations of these products, it is therefore necessary
to install a driver. This is often a formality; you just need to execute
a program called **Installation** or **Setup** on the diskette labelled

"Drivers". With Windows 95, it is also possible to run the automatic detection (**Add/Remove** option from the **Control Panel**), and, if applicable, click on **Have Disk** to install the driver. What installation problems specific to drivers will you encounter, and how do you sort them out? The first problem is identifying the peripheral from amongst the wide range of peripherals and interfaces on your computer. With most modern peripherals, the driver is capable of analysing the content of the PC, of configuring itself as appropriate, and preparing a card so that it matches its own parameters.

Figure 6.3: The Windows automatic detection is a good way of installing a driver

■■■■ Standard or made-to-measure?

It is not necessarily preferable to choose the standard Windows 95 driver. Remember that Windows 95 offers as standard several thousand drivers for many peripherals. As to whether you should prefer these generic drivers to those which are delivered on the manufacturer's diskette, let's just say that, although better tested and more reliable, the Windows 95 driver seldom manages all the capabilities of your interface, and might well therefore limit the scope of your software. Therefore, if you can, use the diskette. At any rate, in many cases (with video acquisition cards, or top-of-the-range graphics cards), Windows 95 will not recognise your peripheral! As far as Windows 3.x is concerned, the problem is solved for you: apart from the printers and screens, this system no longer recognises practically any modern peripheral. You therefore have to install it from a diskette.

The standard Windows driver is not necessarily best
The driver delivered as standard with Windows 95 is admittedly more user-friendly to install and often very reliable, but it doesn't take into account all your peripherals' special features. In many cases, therefore, you should instead use the driver on the diskette, delivered with the hardware, rather than the one from the Windows CD-ROM.

To summarise: in order to optimise the performance of Windows, it is very important to use the manufacturer's driver when the following items are used:

- a sophisticated sound card (AWE 64 for example, made by Creative);

- a scanner;

- a multimedia peripheral (a Miro video acquisition card, for example); or

- a sophisticated graphics card.

You will not gain anything by using a special driver for:

- a mouse;

- a standard VGA card; or

- a bottom-of-the-range network card.

Therefore, the less standard a driver is, the better it is to use the one supplied by the manufacturer. It should be added that certain peripherals work perfectly with Windows drivers in certain situations but not in others. This is the case for a SCSI card driver which is fine in almost all cases when a hard disk is being controlled, but which poses many problems with CD writers. The performance of a PC will often depend on the quality of the driver, so it is important to choose drivers carefully.

Versions and retrieval

You should also watch out for driver faults. If, for example, your 33,600 baud driver does not recognise 33,600 mode, you may have to obtain a new version of the driver to support new functions or correct errors. Retrieving these new versions might be easy or difficult, depending on your situation.

A user connected to the Internet has a considerable advantage. All manufacturers today offer quality services, with a website for downloading software and drivers. Internet users can receive drivers almost instantaneously and change them on a day-to-day basis, while users not connected to the Internet have to go through the manufacturer's technical department and request a diskette by mail. In the best case scenario, this will take two days, but it could take as long as two months. It is always best to ask your dealer if he or she has the latest version in stock. You can always get round this problem by purchasing driver CD-ROMs, but these, whose content is updated once or twice a year, are not necessarily a cure-all. Whatever solution you choose, always have the version number of your current driver to hand; it is pointless to change your driver for an older version.

Obtaining automatic updates over the Internet
Be careful about automatic installation procedures for drivers or "online" updates over the Internet. These are reliable, when telephone lines are reliable. Unfortunately, operators sometimes have problems offering a good link, with the result that you get a half-installed driver, or an upgrade that you don't know is there or not, and which has a high risk of destabilising your system. It is best to download from the Internet site to your hard disk, and then run the driver installation once the whole program has been retrieved.

Figure 6.4: The latest peripherals, such as graphics cards, frequently need drivers

Identifying driver versions

To identify a driver number, start by differentiating between the various types of peripheral driver located in your system. These are those which are loaded when the machine starts up and are stored in the config.sys and autoexec.bat files, and those which are loaded by Windows 95 during its start-up.

Drivers loaded by Windows

For Windows drivers you need to look at the identification sheet for your driver. Open **My Computer** then the **Control Panel**. Click on **System**, then on **Device Manager**. Drop down the list of drivers corresponding to the category of your peripheral (network card, graphics card, etc.) by clicking on the + sign. Select the name of your peripheral, and click on **Properties**, then on the **Driver** tab. Normally, a sheet consisting of the manufacturer's name, the date of manufacture of the driver, and its version number, is displayed. Sometimes, only the date will be shown: this is more than sufficient.

Provided with this information, you can check on the manufacturer's Internet site, or by telephone with their technical support department whether your driver is the most recent version, and, if necessary, whether you can replace it.

Replacing a Windows driver

Once you've got your new driver, installing it is fairly simple. Use the above procedure to access the driver version window and click on **Change Driver**, then on **Select from list**, and on **Have Disk**. If the driver is on your hard disk, use the **Windows Explorer** window to show its path, and then select it. The Windows driver installation procedure is described in detail in Hour 4.

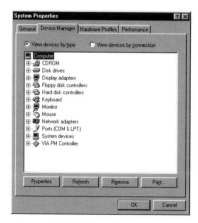

Figure 6.5: All Windows drivers are accessible from the Control Panel, System option

The drivers in the config.sys and autoexec.bat files

In Windows, your PC also uses another procedure for loading drivers: the config.sys and autoexec.bat files. These two files, stored in your PC's C: disk root directory, contain names of drivers which are loaded when the machine is started up.

Upgrading and repairing PCs

Windows needs an additional mechanism for loading drivers in order to preserve compatibility with the old system versions (Windows 3.x, MS-DOS). It is probable that this mechanism will disappear with Windows 98, but meanwhile, you have to use it. Generally, these drivers are concerned with:

- the CD-ROM;
- the hard disk (sometimes);
- some sound cards;
- writers; and
- some Windows functions.

The Windows functions do not concern us; these are managed directly by the system, i.e. the Windows installation procedure modifies or corrects these drivers, if necessary. On the other hand, you will sometimes need to update the drivers for your CD-ROM drive or writer. To find out its version number, carefully watch the start-up of the computer, and the black screen scrolling the text. Each time a driver is loaded, its name, manufacturer and version are displayed. Here again, make a note, check its validity, and, if necessary, get yourself a new version. To install these particular categories of driver, you will need to run a special installation program using the **Run** command from the **Start** menu. The name of the installation program will be shown in the documentation or on the diskette.

Figure 6.6: The autoexec and config files also contain drivers which are more tricky to manage

WINDOWS 95 MULTIMEDIA DRIVERS

System drivers are mainly concerned with multimedia functions and make it possible to display videos, listen to sounds or digitise images. They are therefore dedicated to a system function rather than to managing a peripheral.

These drivers are contained in the **Control Panel**, **Multimedia** option. To look at a list of them, click on the **Advanced** tab. The principle of operation is the same as that of the peripheral drivers. Click on the "+" sign to drop down a driver category. The most important are the MCI Peripherals and the Codec Video Compression Peripherals.

In this menu, you can only drop down a list and look at the names of drivers which are already installed: there's no capability for direct installation here. To install a replacement system driver (to change, for example, from version 3 of Indeo, a video compression program, to Indeo 4) you must run a stand-alone installation program.

Keeping an eye on these drivers in addition to those already mentioned may appear daunting, but you should know that a video error, poor sound quality, or a display fault for example, may be caused by one of them, particularly if you use multimedia or encyclopaedia CD-ROMs.

Broadly speaking, today's computers use the following multimedia drivers:

- Indeo 4.0 from Intel **(www.intel.com)**;
- Vivo **(www.microsoft.com)**;
- MPEG 4 High speed processor **(www.microsoft.com)**;
- Vivo Active Audio Decompressor **(www.microsoft.com)**;
- MCI Microsoft Active Movie **(www.microsoft.com)**; and
- MCI Quicktime for Windows **(www.apple.com)**.

If these names are displayed, it means that your multimedia PC has the most up-to-date drivers. If not, get yourself the up-to-date multimedia drivers from the manufacturers' Internet sites.

PRINT DRIVERS

This hour has not yet discussed printer drivers. These are important, as they affect correct operation and print quality. A faulty driver can cause printing problems such as ripple effects and poor definition.

Figure 6.7: Always consider checking your multimedia drivers

Drivers supplied by Microsoft with Windows 95 are seldom the best, and those from manufacturers are sometimes deficient. Here are a few rules:

- never use the standard Windows driver for your printer, unless the printer is very old, or has just been purchased second-hand;

- if your printer is new, and is a model which has just come out, install the driver delivered on diskette or CD-ROM with the printer;

- if your printer is new, but not the most recent model, try to get the latest version of its driver; and

- if you purchased your printer more than three years ago, check with the manufacturer that a new driver has not come out.

The information relating to the printer driver is accessible from the **Printers** window of the **Control Panel**. Here, nothing is standardised. Right-click on the **Printer** icon, select **Properties** and look for the version number. It is sometimes shown plainly, and is sometimes more tricky to find. For Hewlett Packard printer drivers, for example, you will often find the version number by clicking on **Help**.

To install the new driver for your printer, open the **Printers** window from the **Control Panel**, right-click on the icon for your printer, select **Properties**, and look for the **New Driver** button. Follow the procedure displayed on the screen.

THE FUTURE OF DRIVERS

Although PCI standard and Windows 98 were supposed to do away with configuration and drivers, drivers will be around for some time yet.

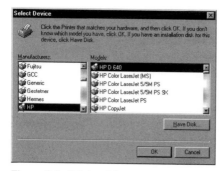

Figure 6.8: Printer drivers are simple, but finding the version number is sometimes complicated

Hour 7

System versions

THE CONTENTS FOR THIS HOUR

- Different forms of update
- Updating in practice
- Particular features of OSR/2
- Activating the FAT32 mode with Windows 95 OSR/2

The most important change you can make to your PC is to upgrade its operating system. Just like Word or WordPerfect, Windows has faults, which you will gradually discover.

You cannot blame the software publisher: it is impossible to put such a complex system on the market, free of any faults, straight away. In addition, besides the design difficulties, it is sometimes the case that spectacular developments in the computing market transform an insignificant section of the software system into an essential part.

This is the case, for example, with the Windows 95 dial-up access card module, a victim of the success of the Internet. Who knew in 1995 that so many users on a planet-wide scale would be equipped with the Internet now? Access to the Internet is made solely through this interface, despite the fact that it is not entirely fault-free.

Another example concerns errors of the type "failure in module x at address xxxx:xxxx". Most often, these indicate that a system or hardware problem is preventing the software from working correctly. It seems that, more and more, software which has been updated (such as the FS95 flight simulator) does not tolerate the faults in the first versions of Windows 95 very well. This is because each new software application which comes out on the market is designed for the latest versions of Windows, using all the functions of the latest version. If the function in question is faulty in the old versions of Windows and that is what is on your PC, then you will get an error message.

In short, for all these reasons and a thousand others, the system on your PC must not remain fixed: it must constantly be renovated, updated and corrected. Unfortunately, this is not simple for all users.

DIFFERENT FORMS OF UPDATE

There is no "miracle version", delivered on a CD-ROM, which would upgrade your entire system. Before describing the various options available, here is a brief reminder of current upgrade terminology according to Microsoft. You will come across the following terms, which are all concerned with a product correction or update:

- Service Pack;
- patch;
- update; and
- OSR.

Why are there so many names for, ultimately, the same objective? The reason is that each update category relates to an action on a precise section of the system. Let us therefore take each of these possibilities one by one.

A Service Pack is a set of small programs which accurately target the updating of certain parts of a system. In other words, the Service Pack does not replace all the Windows components, but only those which need to be updated.

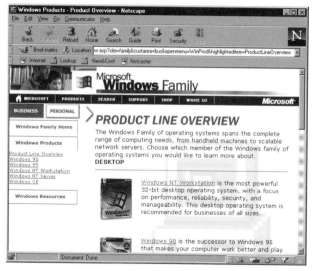

Figure 7.1: The various system updates available from Microsoft's Internet site

A patch is a program which corrects a program. Imagine that the Windows module responsible for printing is faulty; the patch will just correct this program from inside, without replacing it. This allows for rapid updating.

An update is a file which replaces another file. If, for example, the Windows file Kernel32 contains faults, the update consists of a new "Kernel32.exe" module which replaces the previous one. Unlike a patch, an update modifies the version number of the replaced file.

Let us finish with the OSR, a term which appeared with Windows 95 and which should continue with future Microsoft systems, particularly Windows 98. OSR stands for *Operating System Release*. An OSR is a complete new system that replaces all the files in the previous version and corrects as many faults as possible. It is not to be confused with "New versions": Windows 98 is a new version which corrects nothing in Windows 95, but replaces it in full and substitutes a new, totally different, program for it.

It should be added that there are programs which have nothing to do with these four categories and which, nevertheless, correct faults. One example is Microsoft Explorer, which we shall speak about later.

Updates currently available

Below you will find a list of options currently available for updating your PC.

The Windows 95 Service Pack

Dated 3 October 1997.

This first burst of modifications was designed a few months after Microsoft Windows 95 was put on the market. It corrects some of Windows' most annoying faults, and a number of its errors. It also includes a few additional or renovated drivers. When you install this update, the system will indicate to you that its version number is 4.00.950.a.

The advantage of this "release pack" is that it is free and easily accessible by downloading from the Microsoft Internet site. The drawback is that it does not correct everything: it is the OSR/2 which performs the greatest number of corrections, but that has to be paid for!

The "Kernel 32" patch

Dated 6 June 1996.

This is a system component that "fixes" (i.e. corrects) system faults in the software, particularly memory problems. This patch is included in Service Pack 1 and OSR/2; you will probably therefore never need it.

The "ISDN Accelerator Pack 1.1" update

Dated 16 September 1996

Sometimes, an important update hides behind an apparently unnecessary patch. For example, the Microsoft ISDN Accelerator Pack 1.1 is supposed to modify the dial-up access card (the Windows function used for your Internet access) to make it compatible with ISDN telephone lines. In fact, this update corrects the whole dial-up access mechanism, and, consequently, a multitude of faults in this module in its "modem" version. This in turn resolves many Internet connection problems. This update is included in OSR/2.

OSR/2

This is the latest version of Windows and corrects almost all known faults. It is a complete system, which you have to purchase on a CD. Installing this version should solve a good many of the problems and stabilise your PC, although it could still be improved.

When the OSR/2 version is installed, the system will indicate that its version number is 4.00.950.B.

Others

There are other patches and updates, but these are too intricate, limited and task-specific to be worth mentioning here.

When a new component acts as an update

Sometimes a Windows 95 update is concealed behind new components for no apparent reason. A Microsoft program will correct an error in the system for its own requirements, without informing you of its actions.

MSIE 4.0 and OSR/2

It is common knowledge that the installation of Microsoft Explorer 4.0 associated with a Service Pack, or better, with the OSR/2 version of Windows corrects a multitude of faults which OSR/2 alone does not correct. But Explorer 4 must be installed without the Active Desktop (you just need to de-activate the Active Desktop box during installation) since this "PC television channel" device adds additional faults.

DirectX 5.0

With new graphics software and games using video, there has been a need to add more efficient software components to Windows 95 to manage multimedia. This is the case with DirectX 5.0, which, without actually correcting any Windows faults, substantially improves its display capabilities. Theoretically, the majority of recent multimedia applications (marketed since the beginning of 1998) automatically install DirectX 5.0, so it is therefore possible that your system is already up to date (which you can check in the **Control Panel**, **Multimedia** option). If not, installation of the latest version of MSIE 4.0 will also install DirectX 5.0.

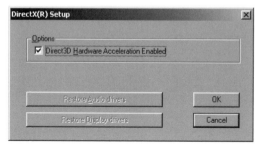

Figure 7.2: DirectX must be installed to improve Windows multimedia functions

UPDATING IN PRACTICE

Here is a list of what it is possible to do to improve your version of Windows 95. Ideally, your PC should have:

- Windows OSR/2;
- DirectX 5.0;
- Microsoft Explorer 4 (MSIE 4); and
- ISDN 1.1 Accelerator Pack.

Even if you have an Internet connection, you should still install MSIE 4, as this tool corrects many Windows faults.

How do you identify your current version of Windows? From **My Computer**, open the **Control Panel**, **System** option. Click on the **General** tab; the Windows version is shown, and if applicable, that of MSIE. If the following text is displayed:

> System
>
> Microsoft Windows 95
>
> 4.00.950.B
>
> IE 4.0 xxxxxxxxxx

this means that everything is fine: OSR/2 is already installed, as is MSIE 4.0 and DirectX 5.0. But if the text is different, for example:

Microsoft Windows 95

4.00.950.a

or some other wording, this means that your PC is equipped with an old version of Windows, or, in the above case, with an old Windows associated with a Service Pack 1. It would therefore be a good idea to install MSIE 4.0 and Windows 95 OSR/2.

How to find these updates

It just remains for you to obtain the update in question. OSR 2 is available in the shops, and you can buy it along with MSIE 4.0 for the price of a CD-ROM. Explorer is also supplied free every month in almost all the specialist magazines.

If you prefer not to pay and would rather make do with Service Packs, you can connect to the Microsoft Internet site at:

http://www.microsoft.com/support/menu/sp/.

Microsoft distributes product updates in the form of corrective patches or new program versions from this website. You can also obtain information on Windows updates. After having selected a product and clicked on **View**, you will see a list of Questions and Answers and will be able to read some details on the system renovation solutions offered by Microsoft.

For even quicker action, connect directly to the "Windows 95 Service Pack" address at:

http://www.microsoft.com/support/products/ windows95/sp/.

All the patches, updates, drivers, and versions we have described in this hour are offered for downloading.

Figure 7.3: The software publishers' Internet sites are the best source of updates. This Figure shows the Microsoft site

To summarise, using our previous list again, you must obtain for yourself:

- Windows OSR/2, by purchasing it from a retailer;

- DirectX 5.0 and Microsoft Explorer 4 (MSIE 4), on CD-ROMs supplied with magazines; and

- ISDN 1.1 Accelerator Pack, from the Microsoft Internet site.

Install these three updates and your PC will function better.

Beta tests

Beta is another name for prototype software. Be careful about participating in beta tests, as programs are likely to be in the process of development and are therefore liable to lock-up a PC, network or hard disk, or even destroy files. They may also be incompatible with certain peripherals. Always install a beta program on a stand-alone computer. In the event of lock-up, the only solution is to reformat your hard disk and resign yourself to losing any programs or files you had stored on it.

PARTICULAR FEATURES OF OSR/2

Now that you have installed your updates, let us turn our attention to a particular feature of the Windows OSR/2 update: the FAT32 mode.

Most hard disks are organised using the FAT16 mode – the mode used on old versions. Yet almost all current PCs use technology capable of adopting the FAT32 mode: a mode of organising the disk which is almost twice as fast.

The first versions of Windows 95 automatically prepared disks in FAT16 mode. The OSR/2 version is, however, capable of managing either the FAT16 or FAT32 mode. Windows 98 works only in FAT32 mode.

You therefore have a choice, with OSR/2, between keeping your current system for organising the hard disk, FAT16 (while being aware that it is less efficient) or upgrading to OSR/2, FAT32.

ACTIVATING THE FAT32 MODE WITH WINDOWS 95 OSR/2

This choice is not easy. Windows 95 OSR/2 does not provide any tools for converting from one mode to the other, so you have to totally reconfigure your machine as we have indicated in the final three hours of this book, in order to change to the FAT32 mode. It is a cumbersome and complicated operation, although it is carried out automatically by Windows 98.

We recommend that you avoid utilities which automatically perform the change from FAT16 to FAT32 without having to reconfigure the entire PC (the utility CVT.EXE for example). Acting on a hard disk at such a low level is always a dangerous solution. If, however, you really want to change to the FAT32 mode, be aware that you will have to:

• back up the whole of your hard disk;

• prepare the entire hard disk using the FDISK command;

• format the disk; and

• install Windows OSR/2.

Figure 7.4: Be careful: changing to the FAT32 mode requires the complete resetting of your PC

Hour 8

Viruses

THE CONTENTS FOR THIS HOUR

- Antivirus actions

- Identifying and dealing with viruses

Computer viruses, even if they are no longer headline news, continue to exist and have become more complex with the development of antivirus software. Viruses can be responsible for:

- destroying the content of a hard disk;

- locking up the PC;

- deleting applications; and

- generating a multitude of incomprehensible and annoying errors.

However, the above four symptoms are not necessarily the sign of a virus being present. We have said this in the preceding hours: software which is too old can cause destruction of files and a PC whose system and hard disks are badly maintained may be the victim of lock–ups and unexplained errors. Apart from the traditional antivirus software, how do you know if your PC has a virus? Let us begin by learning where a virus comes from, and where it does not come from:

- often from a diskette loaned by a friend;

- seldom from a file downloaded over the Internet;

- almost always from a pirated, copied and exchanged game;

- almost never from a document (text or spreadsheet);

- never from an image;

- never from a magazine CD-ROM; and

- never from installation diskettes for reputable software.

These propagation rules are due to the actual mechanism of the virus, since its principle of operation is fairly simple.

A bad joke
You may be sent virus- infected software by electronic mail so that, when you run the program, your PC is infected. Therefore always be suspicious of programs sent to your electronic mailbox by unknown correspondents.

The virus is a piece of program with a dual objective: its first is propagation, its second is action (destruction of data, for example). Propagation involves infecting the maximum number of PCs, whereas action involves satisfying the ego of the person who invented the virus.

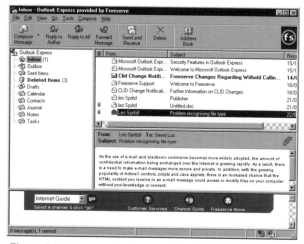

Figure 8.1: Beware of unknown files attached to electronic mail

To fulfil these two objectives, the virus is as small as possible. In this way it can conceal itself on a hard disk, and attempt to "cling on" to one of the programs it contains. Once infected, the program will act as a virus multiplier . Each time it runs, it will create a copy of the virus, which will infect another program, and so on. All it takes to infect your PC is for you to run the program.

The basic rule is this: the less open your PC is to external "unknown" virus, the less vulnerable it is. You will be a victim of viruses if you exchange programs too frequently, but never or almost never if you use official software, and if you do nothing but receive or send data. Antivirus measures therefore exist to protect users.

ANTIVIRUS ACTIONS

The best antivirus measure you can take is to stop the virus infecting your PC in the first place. To help you, here are a few pieces of advice:

- Pirate software copies may well be infected with a virus present on the hard disk of whoever made the copy.

- Official software, sold by a software publisher, is never infected.

- To avoid infecting your computer, never copy "small programs" (games or utilities) onto your PC. By all means install new programs, but use reliable sources, such as CD-ROMs supplied with magazines.

IDENTIFYING AND DEALING WITH VIRUSES

It is all very well learning how to prevent a virus. But what if one already exists on your hard disk? How do you know it is there? The typical symptoms of an infection are:

- an installation program asks for diskette "number 2", and interrupts itself by displaying the message Error on diskette number 2: this is because the virus was already on the PC and has interfered with your diskettes during the installation procedure;

- the PC refuses to start up with the message Boot Sector faulty or damaged; or

- the number of scrambled File Table messages increases.

Diagnosis

- In almost all cases, diskette number 2 will be damaged by a virus which was already present on your machine before the installation of Windows 95. This generally occurs on the second diskette, because your user information is written on this diskette.

- Boot problems are symptomatic of a previously installed virus which has begun its destructive action. These viruses attack the sector which boots the system when the machine is switched on, thus preventing the PC from starting up.

- Scrambled File Table or File Length Error messages relate to viruses which destroy the structure of the files contained on the hard disk. They are somewhere on the disk, and have to be found and eradicated.

Sorting out the problem

A few words of advice for fending off viruses are as follows:

- Several viruses may be causing your problem. The best solution is to use an antivirus program to analyse your computer before starting an installation.

- Write-protect all your diskettes: push back the protective tab in the upper left corner. A write-protected diskette cannot be the victim of a virus attack. A warning message may be displayed during the installation phase, but the procedure will reach completion without any problem. However, this is a temporary solution, which will not eliminate any virus present on the computer.

- When viruses are installed in the Boot sector of your hard disk, first try restarting the PC by putting a system diskette into the floppy disk drive, then getting rid of them with the command FDISK / MBR. This solution is unfortunately also temporary. This is because the virus may be removed from the startup sector, while remaining active and concealed elsewhere on the hard disk. In other cases, it is always present somewhere, on the hard disk. In addition, the file structure which is damaged remains so and could well cause subsequent new errors.

Your first action, once the virus attack has been fended off and the system stabilised, will therefore be to:

- get rid of suspect diskettes;

- clean all the PC's disks with antivirus software; and

• use the ScanDisk command to repair the file structure errors (which will probably destroy hundreds of files and programs).

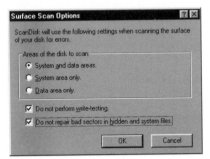

Figure 8.2: Use ScanDisk to repair the damage caused by a virus

This is a temporary solution. It will make it possible to back up all your documents (which are not subject to virus attacks), and then carry out the complete reconfiguration of your computer as described in the second part of this book.

Hour 9

Solutions

THE CONTENTS FOR THIS HOUR

- Repair and installation
- Viruses
- Register bases

You will sometimes encounter insurmountable problems when maintaining your PC. Here, therefore, are a few questions and answers for optimising performance, repairing your PC, and sorting out problems.

REPAIR AND INSTALLATION

▄▄▄ Activating the self-repair function

If Windows 95 stops with no explanation, behaves strangely, or produces numerous system errors, run the installation program from the CD-ROM. The Installation Wizard will automatically check all the files, identify those which are damaged, and repair them.

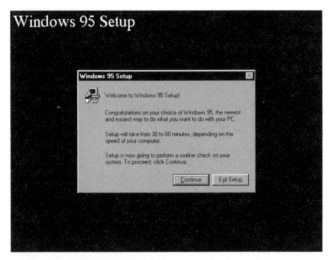

Figure 9.1: The Installation Wizard is able to repair the Windows register bases

▄▄▄ Hard disk error

If your hard disk is causing problems, try using the ScanDisk utility to check it.

▬▬▬ Windows stops after the blue startup screen (1)

A screen for an antivirus program is hidden behind the Windows 95 logo. Remove your antivirus software from the autoexec.bat or config.sys file.

▬▬▬ Windows stops after the blue startup screen (2)

Your graphics card driver is not suitable. Try starting Windows while keeping the **F5** or **F8** keys pressed down at startup, and change the driver.

▬▬▬ Windows stops after the blue startup screen (3)

If you are equipped with an ATI Graphics Ultra Pro (Mach32) graphics card, get the latest up-to-date driver and install it.

▬▬▬ An installation program does not work from a diskette

Close all Windows programs, remove the "32-bit" file mode (**Control Panel**, **System** option), and restart the installation program.

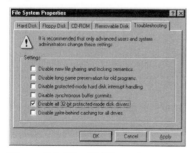

Figure 9.2: The 32-bit mode can sometimes give problems during installation

ScanDisk no longer responds

Wait for three minutes: ScanDisk should give control back to you.
If not, change to MS-DOS Commands mode by dropping down
the **Start** menu and selecting the **MS-DOS Commands** option,
then type "scandisk/IS".

*Figure 9.3: ScanDisk has a secret function for avoiding
system halts*

Windows Setup stops during hardware detection

Try shutting down your computer properly (do not use
Ctrl+Alt+Del or the **Reset** button), wait a few seconds and switch
it on again.

OSR/2 system problem

A frequent problem on Windows 95 OSR/2 computers is that the
peripheral drivers are loaded twice. If you encounter this problem,
start Windows by pressing **F5**, go to the **Device Manager** in the
Control Panel, and delete all the duplicate drivers. This operation
should resolve your problems.

How to delete Internet Explorer 4 after a failed installation

The installation of MSIE 4 sometimes ends in failure. It then becomes impossible, not only to delete it, but also to reinstall it. Fortunately, a magic tool solves this problem – the utility "ieremove.exe", which forces the uninstallation of MSIE and makes it possible to then restart the installation procedure. To run "ieremove.exe", go into **MS-DOS Commands** mode with the **Start** menu, select the **MS-DOS** option, then type "cd \windows\system" in order to go to the directory containing the utility. Type "Ieremove /R" and reinstall.

VIRUSES

Viruses may sometimes be installed in the startup sector of the hard disk.

An antivirus trick

When a virus is installed in the startup sector of your hard disk, first try getting rid of the virus with the command FDISK /MBR. Unfortunately this solution is inadequate and temporary. This is because the virus may be removed from the Master Boot Record, while remaining active and concealed elsewhere on the hard disk. It is therefore preferable, in addition, to run an antivirus program, back up the content of the disk, then reformat it at low level and reinstall everything.

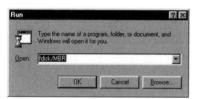

Figure 9.4: The only solution in the event of a serious virus attack is complete reformatting

▇▇▇▇ Undocumented system tool functions

From DOS 5 and higher versions, system utilities are provided with highly efficient undocumented functions for repairing a Master Boot Record:

- FDISK /PRI: directly creates a primary partition;

- FDISK /EXT: directly creates an extended partition;

- FDISK /LOG: directly creates a logical partition; and

- FDSIK /MBR: rewrites the Master Boot Record (the bootstrap) while leaving the partition tables intact.

With Windows 3, use the function MIRROR /MBR before typing FDISK /MBR. In this way, you back up your partition table in a file called "PARTNSAV.FIL" to be copied onto a diskette which you can restore later using the following method: Using the command UNFORMAT /PARTN, insert the diskette containing "PARTNSAV.FIL" and the Master Boot Record information will be restored.

REGISTER BASES

Register base problems are the scourge of the PC user. It is sometimes necessary to restore or repair them at regular intervals in order to maintain the stability of the system. For your convenience, we recommend that you use the software described in the Appendix of this book in order to easily repair the register bases. Meanwhile, here are a few practical words of advice.

▇▇▇▇ Removing a register base error

In the event of the Register Base Error message being displayed, restart your computer, leaving the **F8** key pressed. Select the **MS-DOS Commands** mode only, and go to the Windows directory, using the MS-DOS Command cd c: \Windows. Type "regedit /e savebutt.reg". The message "Exporting file" is displayed, sometimes associated with an error message. Then, type "attrib system.dat -r -

s -h" then "ren system.dat system.old". Type "regedit /e savebutt.reg" again. Normally a new, working, register base is recreated. Otherwise, reinstall Windows!

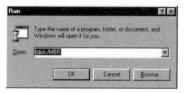

Figure 9.5: The utility regedit.exe, delivered with Windows, makes it possible to explore and modify your register bases

Register base retrieval

Windows 95 stores information about your computer's hardware and software in the System.dat file, located in the Windows directory. Two backup copies of the System.dat file are regularly automatically created. The installation creates one backup copy of the register base in the root directory, called System.1st. Another backup copy (called System.dao) is created in the Windows directory. This backup copy is a copy of the register base before the last restart. Each time you start Windows 95 successfully, the file System.dat is copied to the file System.dao. These files are hidden and read-only. To display them, you must therefore remove the **Hidden Files** option by right-clicking, **Properties** option, on the icon for the Windows directory. In the event of a problem, you can copy these files, renaming them "*.dat", into the Windows directory in order to retrieve a working register base.

Take care with modifications

If the register base is damaged, numerous errors may occur; or your computer might not start up correctly. The modifications you make in the Control Panel when you are trying to sort out the problem may cause the damaged System.dat file to be rewritten on top of the System.dao file, thus making both files faulty. Therefore consider protecting the original System.dat file (by renaming it System.pro, for example) before performing any action on the drivers or the configuration.

Part 2

Starting again from scratch

Hour 10

Warnings and preparation

THE CONTENTS FOR THIS HOUR

- Preparatory work

- Configuration

- Creating a startup diskette

If you do not take proper care of your PC, you will soon find that the hard disk becomes cluttered with unwanted data and the system crashes more and more frequently, making your computer almost unusable. In this case, there may only be one solution: to start again from scratch.

The first problem is knowing how to assess when it is necessary to start again, or if emergency measures can still be applied. In broad terms, it is necessary to start again from scratch when the PC:

- constantly produces system errors, which cannot be resolved by reinstalling Windows;

- constantly suffers hard disk errors which ScanDisk can no longer sort out;

- locks up for no reason, all the time, including when you have cleaned the disk or installed a new version of Windows; or

- displays register base errors every five minutes, despite the register bases having been restored with the Windows installation.

Figure 10.1: If you get more and more errors, you should reinstall

If your PC has been damaged to this extent, no further treatment can do anything for it. The accumulation of minor faults has permanently destabilised the system, and damaged all or part of the organisation of the hard disk. The majority of repair utilities will be of no use, as small fragments will always remain on the disk whatever operations you carry out. Worse, if viruses are the cause of your problems, they can sometimes survive ScanDisk or Format type procedures. In short, you will have to start again.

You will gain from this: many users have noticed a significant improvement in their PC's performance as a result of this renovation.

What does it consist of? First, a series of quite cumbersome operations, which will take you a lot of time. The aim is to return your computer to its basic state, almost that of the day it left the factory, and to prepare it, as your dealer did before delivering it to you.

You will thus benefit from obtaining a renovated, rejuvenated PC, which will run like clockwork, just like the day you switched it on for the first time.

Complete renovation of the content of a PC consists of:

- resetting the hard disk to zero, identical to its state when it left the factory: this is known as "basic" formatting;

- preparing the hard disk for the system at an advanced level: this process is known as partitioning, and uses the FDISK utility;

- formatting the hard disk to make it compatible with the system;

- reinstalling the system (Windows 95);

- reinstalling the components of Windows 95;

- reinstalling certain drivers for your hardware;

- reinstalling your applications software; and

- reinstalling your files.

As you can see, this will take some time, certainly more than the three hours we will devote to this explanation.

You should reset your PC using the latest version of Windows 95.

It is absolutely essential that you obtain a Windows 95 OSR/ 2 to reset your computer. The old versions have too many problems and errors to be corrected.

If you have not got a CD-ROM of your old version of Windows, the one which was installed when your PC was supplied to you, you must get the Windows OSR/2 version for a more recent PC, which will be more expensive. This is unfortunate, but that is how it is: the OSR/2 update verifies the presence of an old system. If absent, the installation will not be able to continue.

If you have an old version of Windows 3.X, you can use it for installing a Windows 95 OSR/2 update.

PREPARATION

Keep it in mind that, in order to reinitialise, you are going to destroy absolutely everything the PC contains: configuration, system, utilities, and also information on the drivers. Everything will be deleted. You should therefore take a few preparatory measures before resetting your PC.

Backing up everything that needs to be backed up

Before reinitialising, you should back up files you will be reinstalling later, such as word-processing files, spreadsheets, images and any type of document you need.

As a general rule, back up only what is strictly necessary, and abandon any file which could be retrieved from another PC or a storage medium.

Remember to clean files before backing them up.

There is no point backing up damaged files. Scrambled file problems and other structural or content errors may be copied at the same time as the backup, with the result that, when you reinstall your PC, the errors would still be there in the backed-up documents. Before transferring your files to a backup, therefore, you should carry out a rapid analysis of the structure of the disk and the files using ScanDisk, abandoning all files described by ScanDisk as being permanently damaged.

Figure 10.2: Remember to clean files before backing them up

Abandoning what needs to be renovated

To avoid saving old viruses, do not back up any file (with the exception of the programs contained in the installation diskette) with the extension ".com", ".exe", "ovl", "dll" or "drv". These executable files are liable to be infected. Even the utilities you need so much must be either reinstalled from your original diskettes or CD-ROM, or downloaded from the Internet.

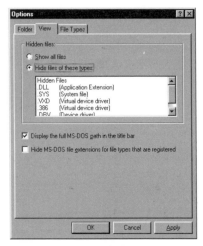

Figure 10.3: It is pointless to copy executable files

Obviously, do not keep any programs. All these must be reinstalled from their original diskettes or the initialisation CD-ROM.

CONFIGURATION

You will be advised in some books to back up your computer's register bases and configuration files (the .ini files and the .dat files in the c:\windows directory) with a view to simplifying the reinstallation. This is a clever idea, since, in theory, by copying the old system files which were already prepared, the information relating to the PC's peripherals (which will not change) is recovered and a complete reconfiguration is avoided.

Our point of view on this subject is different. On the basis that some malfunctions of your old configuration could very well be generated by damaged system or initialisation files, recovering these files could reproduce errors when you reinstall Windows.

Another solution is to note down on a sheet of paper all the parameters for your PC before reinstalling. Running through the **Control Panel**, **System** option, **Device Manager** tab, explore each peripheral and component of the PC, one by one, and note down the information contained in the **Resources** tab. Of all the information, IRQ, DMA and input/output addresses are the most important.

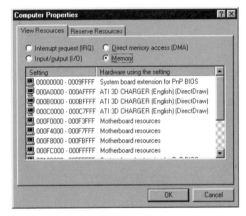

Figure 10.4: Noting down all the resources for your peripherals

Creating a startup diskette

The last, very important, step is the creation of a startup diskette. Remember that, in reformatting your disk, you will destroy its entire contents and, by the same token, you will delete the system software and the utilities it contains. In order to access your PC and prepare it, you have to insert a diskette in its drive. The first point to remember is that the diskette must contain the system, that is, be formatted with the command:

    C:>Format A: /S

You must then copy onto this diskette the following utilities:

- FDISK.EXE;
- FORMAT.COM; and
- DEBUG.EXE.

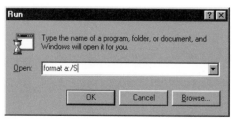

Figure 10.5: Creating a startup diskette using the FORMAT option

You will find them in the **C:\Windows\Command** directory of your hard disk. To copy them on to the startup diskette, type:

> **copy c:\windows\command\fdisk.exe a:**

> **copy c:\windows\command\format.com a:**

> **copy c:\windows\command\debug.exe a:**

The startup diskette must also allow operation of the CD-ROM since the Windows system is delivered on this medium. You must therefore copy the files necessary for operation of the CD-ROM drive. Therefore copy the autoexec.bat and config.sys files onto the diskette using the command:

> **copy c:\autoexec.bat a:**

> **copy c:\config.sys a:**

Be careful, as the paths contained in these files correspond to the location of your programs on the hard disk. You must therefore modify them to make them point to the floppy disk drive. Therefore, the following config.sys file:

```
REM == ECS IDE CD-ROM Install Modification -
Begin =======

DEVICEHIGH=C:\ECSCDIDE.SYS /D:ECSCD003

REM == ECS IDE CD-ROM Install Modification - End
========

device=C:\WINDOWS\COMMAND\display.sys
con=(EGA,,1)

country=033,850,C:\WINDOWS\COMMAND\country.sys
```

will become:

```
REM == ECS IDE CD-ROM Install Modification -
Begin =======

DEVICEhigh=ECSCDIDE.SYS /D:ECSCD003

REM == ECS IDE CD-ROM Install Modification - End
========

device=display.sys con=(ega,,1)

country=033,850, country.sys
```

The same applies for the following Autoexec.bat file:

```
LH    C:\WINDOWS\COMMAND\MSCDEX.EXE    /
d:MSCD0001 /M:50 /L

mode con codepage prepare=((850)

C:\WINDOWS\COMMAND\EGA.CPI)

mode con codepage select=850

keyb uk,,C:\WINDOWS\COMMAND\keyboard.sys
```

which will become:

```
LH MSCDEX.EXE /D:MSCD0001 / M:50 /L

mode con codepage prepare=((850) EGA.CPI)

mode con codepage selec=850

keyb uk,, keyboard.sys
```

Also copy the driver for the CD-ROM drive by means of the command:

copy c:\windows\command\mscdex.exe a:

You must also copy the system driver for the CD-ROM, invoked by the file "config.sys". To identify it, look for a line of the type:

```
REM ===== ECS IDE CD-ROM Install Modification -
Begin ========

DEVICEHIGH=C:\ECSCDIDE.SYS /D:ECSCD003

REM ===== ECS IDE CD-ROM Install Modification -
End ========
```

The above case concerns an IDE-type CD-ROM drive, initialised by the file "ECSDIDE.SYS" contained in the root of the disk.

Copy this file using the command:

copy c:\ecsdide.sys a:

Theoretically, your startup diskette is now created: in theory only, since you are not beyond making a minor operational error. A word of advice therefore, before rushing into reinstallation: check that this diskette works by stopping your machine, inserting it into the floppy disk drive, and switching the PC on again. Do not worry about any error messages which might be displayed. The main thing is that the diskette works and finishes with the prompt "C:>" on a black screen.

Figure 10.6: The startup diskette must be checked and should display the above prompt

Also check that you can read the content of a CD-ROM, by inserting it in the drive.

Hour 11

Formatting

THE CONTENTS FOR THIS HOUR

- Formatting proceedures

- Partitioning or booting

- Software formatting

Now you can start to reinitialise your PC via a number of steps for preparing the hard disk. This is known as formatting. Switch off your machine, insert the startup diskette into its drive, and start up again. In doing so, you will destroy the old data on your PC.

FORMATTING PROCEDURES

Formatting involves preparing a hard disk or magnetic medium in order for it to be recognised by a standard. To be more precise, it involves making the hard disk supplied by the manufacturer compatible with your operating system.

This is what the format is, an organisation of a magnetic surface in tracks, and a division of tracks into sectors, for the purpose of compatibility with an operating system. The reason this is not done in the factory is that each computer manufacturer or operating system supplier chooses for themselves how tracks and sectors are organised. Of course, PC manufacturers all choose the same format: Microsoft Windows, which is delivered with their machine. But there are other machines: the Macintosh, computers with a UNIX system, and several others. There are a number of types of formatting, as follows:

- basic formatting;
- partitioning or booting; and
- software formatting.

These three types of format are stacked, and make use of one another. Thus, basic formatting is the so-called factory format: its function is to start from a smooth magnetic surface and mark out a track and sectors on that surface. We shall use one of the variants of this format, which is highly practical since it is the only one to guarantee the total erasure of the content of the hard disk.

On top of this factory format, a basic "booting" or partitioning formatting is added, which consists solely of preparing the first sectors of each hard disk and dividing the medium into "partitions". The basic intelligence of your computer (the BIOS) is composed of a set of small programs, which run automatically each time the machine is started. It is one of these, for example, which displays the breakdown of the memory when the PC starts up. One of these

BIOS programs uses its own method for recognising the PC's hard disks, assigning them a letter (C, D, E, etc.), in order to know whether it must go and fetch the system from one of them for starting up, and, if applicable, assesses whether certain "physical" disks are divided into a number of "logical" disks. In other words, the C disk may very well be divided into a number of "logical" disks, C, D, E, a little like the compartments of a railway carriage.

Once prepared by this method, the hard disk can be "formatted" for the system, since the above two preparatory steps only cause "basic grooves" to be marked out on the disk: the tracks and the sectors. These spaces are designed to receive "raw" data, and must therefore be prepared for management by an operating system (Windows 95) with its sophisticated requirements. This is because the operating system has more advanced requirements. It manages a file system (the organisation method which makes it possible to say that file X is in area Y of the hard disk), to which it assigns characteristics (name, length, date, time).

Now you can see why it is important to keep your PC in good working order. If you format your system incorrectly, your files will be damaged, while if the partitioning is poor, the system will no longer start up.

Basic formatting

In the past, hard disk or PC manufacturers offered PC users "basic" functions identical to those which were carried out on leaving the factory production line. These have almost disappeared. True basic formatting is now an industrial process which is done only when the disk comes into existence. The majority of so-called "basic" formatting procedures, therefore, are really total formatting routines. These routines do not organise the medium at the magnetic level, but just write and read the sectors of the disk, making sure that they are completely empty and functional. These routines therefore remain the only ones capable of totally erasing a hard disk and its content while the majority of other formatting tools just restructure the tracks, leaving marks on the disk. They are therefore good for permanently deleting data or viruses. It should also be pointed out that the FORMAT command, applied to a diskette, is a basic formatting procedure as well.

 Factory formatting
What was in the past called "basic formatting" no longer exists on current disks. Factory formatting is carried out once and is designed to last for the entire life of the disk.

How do you carry out basic disk formatting?

The basic formatting procedure is not the most simple to carry out. It is nevertheless important, since it alone will allow permanent resolution of all the malfunctions caused by magnetic failures of the hard disk. It should be pointed out, however, that basic formatting is not absolutely necessary. The following steps will satisfactorily clean the disk in 99% of cases.

To start the procedure, you must use the "Debug" utility, which serves as an interface for activating the "basic format" function hidden in the disk controller. All you need to do is type the command G=XXXX:X.

```
Microsoft(R) Windows 95
    (C)Copyright Microsoft Corp 1981-1996.

C:\WINDOWS>debug
-G=C8000:CCC
```

Figure 11.1: The Debug command activates the basic formatting procedure

The problem is the "XXXX:X". This represents a program start address, and is different on all PCs. You must therefore find it in the documentation for your hard disk controller (or motherboard if the latter incorporates this function). Here are a few examples, starting with the information to be given after the G=XXXX:

- on a Western digital controller, the address is XXXX:5;

- on an Adaptec, it is XXXX:CCC;

- on a Seagate, it is XXXX:5.

These three cases fit the characteristics of the majority of recently sold PCs. As for the XXXX, the address will probably be C800, or perhaps D800. The activation of a basic formatting procedure will therefore be, for example, in many Adaptec controller-based configurations:

G=C800:CCC.

It really becomes more complicated after this, since the program will ask you many questions relating to the characteristics of the hard disk. Refer to the user documentation for more information.

The manufacturer's software
The majority of manufacturers offer their own basic formatting software. If you can, try to obtain them (for example, from their Internet site): the interface is more user-friendly, and the formatting is simplified.

Partitioning or booting

Partitioning is simpler. We will prepare everything using the FDISK command, which fortunately works with menus, and is therefore clearly expressed. Restart the machine with your startup diskette, and type **FDISK** at the prompt.

FDISK
Only the Windows 95 OSR/2 FDISK.EXE offers to partition your hard disk in wide mode (more than 2 Gb of data), and in FAT32 mode. If your PC was previously equipped with

an old version of Windows and you created your startup diskette with this old system, then the diskette will be equipped with the old FDISK. It will therefore not offer the FAT32 and Wide Disk modes. One solution is to install Windows OSR/2 in order to create a startup diskette, then repeat everything from Hour 10, although this will take a considerable time. A simpler solution would be to ask your dealer or a friend equipped with the latest version of Windows to create a startup diskette for you, containing the correct version of FDISK.

```
                      Microsoft Windows 95
                     Fixed Disk Setup Program
              (C)Copyright Microsoft Corp. 1983 - 1995

                          FDISK Options

Current fixed disk drive: 1

Choose one of the following:

1. Create DOS partition or Logical DOS Drive
2. Set active partition
3. Delete partition or Logical DOS Drive
4. Display partition information


Enter choice: [1]




Press Esc to exit FDISK
```

Figure 11.2: Booting and partitioning are carried out using FDISK

A number of questions appear on the screen. The first is the most important.

By replying **Yes** to the first question, you will be activating the FAT32 mode, which was touched upon in earlier chapters. This will make your PC more efficient and prepare it better if you wish to upgrade to Windows 98.

Your computer has a disk greater than 512 Mb. This version of Windows includes improved management for large disks, which allows better use of the disk space on large drives, and formatting of a disk greater than 2 Gb as a single drive.

In the next window, entitled FDISK Options, select **Create DOS partition** or **Logical DOS Drive**.

In the next screen, select **Create Primary DOS Partition**. To the question: Should all available disk space be reserved, reply **Yes**. Return to the main menu, and request **Set active partition** by pressing **1**. FDISK will then start to work.

Figure 11.3: Creating a DOS partition using FDISK

Why does a hard disk appear to offer less space than indicated in its documentation?
The Windows and DOS partitioning software, FDISK, calculates the size of a disk to the base 2. In other words, one megabyte is equal to 1,048,576 bytes. The manufacturers, however, calculate the megabyte to the base 10, that is one million bytes. This difference is essentially due to the historical differences between the software and hardware industries. Strangely, the CHKDSK program also calculates the space on a disk to the base 10 (that is 1 Mb = 1,000,000 bytes), whereas FDISK calculates to the base 2.

You can return to the **Create DOS partition** [...] menu and create one or more drives in the DOS extended partition. It is up to you to decide whether you want a single drive, that is, a single disk over the entire available capacity, or more than one, that is, one disk divided into a number of compartments.

SOFTWARE FORMATTING

All that remains is for you to carry out software formatting using the FORMAT command. One of the simplest operations, you just need to type the command **FORMAT /C: /S /V**.

In this line, /C: means that the hard disk C must be formatted, installing a bootstrap for the system, while the /V command indicates that you have to assign a volume name to the hard disk.

Now that you have formatted your disk, you are in a position to install Windows and software programs. This is dealt with in the final chapter.

Hour 12

Installing Windows and software programs

THE CONTENTS FOR THIS HOUR

- Installation of Windows
- Installation of software programs and documents

Now that you have cleaned up your hard disk, you can start to reinstall your programs. Switch off your PC, insert the Windows 98 OSR/2 disk in the CD-ROM drive and switch on again.

INSTALLATION OF WINDOWS

Change the prompt to the letter for the CD-ROM, and type **"Install"**.
You will be asked for certain information, including the Windows
serial number, which is written on the back of the CD case.

Select the "default" installation mode. We do not recommend
customised installation, which is too complicated. The "default" mode
is simple and very comprehensive. The majority of your peripherals
will be detected automatically, and their drivers installed.

Once the system is finally installed, a few checks are necessary.
First, you will need to make sure that all your peripherals are
recognised (such as modems and scanners), by looking at the Device
Manager's list, in the **System** option of the **Control Panel**. Here
are the problems which you may be faced with.

*Figure 12.1: You will need to check the System tab
once Windows has been installed*

Yellow exclamation marks in front of a peripheral name

If you get yellow exclamation marks in front of your peripheral
name, it means that two drivers are installed for the same peripheral.

Delete the one which is marked with a yellow exclamation mark. If
this deletion causes a malfunction, trigger a new hardware detection
using the **Add New Hardware** function in the **Control Panel**.

*Figure 12.2: You must add undetected peripherals
with the Add New Hardware function*

Problems with advanced peripherals

You may find a fault with one of the following types of advanced
peripheral (this list is not exhaustive):

- top-of-range sound card (AWE32);

- high-speed graphics card (Matrox, STB);

- graphics accelerator card (3D FX);

- scanner; or

- video acquisition card.

If this is the case, start the special installation procedure delivered
with your peripheral or, if applicable, that of an update acquired
later (always install the latest known driver). Between each
procedure, consider restarting your computer, returning to the
Control Panel, **System** option, and checking that no peripheral
has been assigned an exclamation mark. If applicable, delete the
least suitable driver (the standard Windows VGA driver for a
graphics card, for example).

Deleting standardised drivers

If your PC is equipped with a modem, or if Windows has detected a printer, the standard system drivers will have been installed as a priority. Replace them with the drivers delivered by the modem or printer manufacturer.

Refining the configuration

Here are a few tips for refining the Windows configuration.

The display

By default, Windows has been installed for a display in 16-colour, 640 by 480-pixel mode. However, the majority of screens offer a 256-colour, 800 by 600-pixel mode, which is better to use. Right-click on the screen background, select the **Properties** option, **Configuration** tab, select "800 by 600 pixels", and drop down to "256 colours". Do not give in to the temptation of selecting 65,000 or 16 million colours, which waste a lot of processor power.

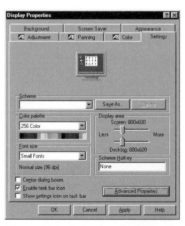

Figure 12.3: Selecting the 256-colour mode, which is less greedy in terms of machine power

The virtual memory

By default, the Windows virtual memory, accessible from the **System** option, **Performance** tab, of the **Control Panel**, is installed on your C disk. It risks fragmenting it, and you are advised to assign it to another disk, if your PC is equipped with one: the D disk for example. Click on **Virtual Memory**, select the box **Let me specify my own virtual memory settings**, select **Maximum** and drive letter "**D**".

Graphics performance

Still in the **System** menu, **Performance** tab, of the **Control Panel**, click on the **Graphics** option and set the hardware acceleration to full. Your graphics card will be used to its fullest capabilities. If you see display errors, it is because the driver is not suitable. Try, therefore, installing the driver corresponding to your graphics card.

To do this, look for the name of its processor set in the documentation, or its exact reference, click on **Add New Hardware** in the **Control Panel**, ask to select from a list, **Graphics Card** option, and select the correct driver.

▆▆▆ Installing MSIE 4.X

Complete this installation by installing Microsoft Explorer 4.X (the X for the latest version available), which you can get, among other places, from CD-ROMs supplied with magazines.

Install everything, with the exception of the Active Desktop, which you must de-activate.

Figure 12.4: Installing Microsoft Explorer

INSTALLATION OF SOFTWARE PROGRAMS AND DOCUMENTS

You are now ready to reinstall all your software programs. For this, use the installation procedure associated with the **Customised** option. The installation methods are described in Hour 4. Simply bear in mind the following rules:

- install only what is useful; avoid superfluous clipart or tutorial type items;

- avoid excessive fonts: no more than100 in total;

- avoid gadgets, like the Office 97 Startup Bar;

- when the software proposes replacing one file with a more recent one, agree; and

- install all the software programs in the directory **c:\programs\files**.

Retrieve all your documents from a backup, and copy them into a Document directory, if possible on a disk other than the Windows one.

Reinstall your applications software, if possible in a directory other than the Windows one and on another disk drive.

YOUR PC IS NOW IN TIP-TOP CONDITION!

Your PC should now be in tip-top condition, with up-to-date drivers for your peripherals and a clean hard disk. But remember that maintaining your computer is an ongoing job. Therefore start by backing up your register bases and configuration files (see Hour 9), defragmenting and examining your disk with ScanDisk (see Hour 3). Do not forget to check your drivers (see Hour 6). Also, in a few days, consider cleaning your unnecessary files and uninstalling those things you will not be needing any more (see Hour 5). In short, start again from the beginning.

Appendix

Useful software

All the operations described in this book, and many others, can also be carried out with specialised software. The function of this software is to simplify, automate, and improve Windows maintenance procedures. They have to be paid for (that is their shortcoming), but are very powerful. Some of them, such as Nuts and Bolts for example, perform very sophisticated register base cleaning. It is strongly recommended that you equip yourself with one of them.

DR SOLOMON'S ANTIVIRUS SOFTWARE

The range of Dr Solomon's antivirus software, available for DOS, Windows 3.X, Windows 95, Windows NT, OS/2, UNIX, Macintosh and Netware, offers you a high level of protection.

This tool supports the multitasking capabilities of Windows. That is, it is capable of scanning and repairing your hard disk in the background while you are working.

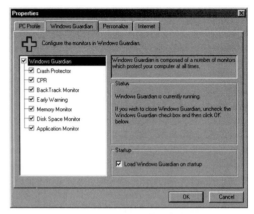

Figure A.1: Use specialized accessories to clean your PC

The WINGUARD module monitors each file and the disks. It has the following capabilities:

- it prevents infection by stopping the execution of infected programs;

- it checks the startup sectors of each diskette used;

- it has a function for remote update via the Internet; and

- it has a function for feedback of warnings, via modem, fax, network message, e-mail and pager.

Software publisher: ABSoft.

Test configuration: Cyrix 166, 32 Mb RAM, 1.6 Gb DD EIDE.

THE "NORTON" SERIES

Utilities, Crashguard Deluxe, and Uninstall are the three main products of this series of well-known utilities, designed by Symantec. The aim of this set of programs is to sort out all configuration, maintenance and update problems which a user may encounter. These utilities are very efficient and include a few useful features such as the basic formatting tool. On the other hand, these tools are sometimes too powerful and are not necessary for everyone. Here are a few details on these products:

- the Norton Utilities is a set of utilities for checking and managing the correct operation of the hard disk;

- Crashguard Deluxe attempts to sort out system and register base error problems, and, if necessary, makes it possible to recover a software program before it crashes or locks up the system; and

- Norton Uninstall Deluxe is a very good uninstallation accessory which has the ability to remove everything from a hard disk, including certain libraries which have a tendency to accumulate in the Windows 95 System directory.

Software publisher: Symantec.

Test configuration: Cyrix 166, 32 Mb RAM, 1.6 Gb DD EIDE.

NUTS AND BOLTS

Nuts and Bolts is the name for a set of utilities essential for maintaining, protecting and servicing your PC. Available on a single CD, the program gathers together tools for preventing accidents, for optimising performance, and for cleaning the disk and the system. One of the most spectacular utilities is "Anticrash", which monitors the system. If an application crashes, or if Windows hangs or locks up, "Anticrash" keeps a system stable. System failures are not prevented, but neutralised. It is possible to continue working after an application has crashed.

But because a failure can never really be avoided, there are also accessories for recovering ruined disks or damaged files, and even register bases. The majority of these utilities are accessible to everyone. They use the Windows "Wizards" to simplify operations. Thus, the Shortcut Wizard takes care of examining all available shortcuts on a system, and, if necessary, destroying or repairing those which no longer correspond to any file. Better still, the Register Base Wizard deletes all entries which have become unnecessary and cleans the others.

There are other features as well, such as the Windows Monitoring Panel, which, at a single go, displays a multitude of information updated in real time (the time, instantaneous power, available space or fragmentation), or System Analysis, which identifies, compares, and checks each component in a PC, from the PCI bus to the memory, through the processor speed.

Figure A.2: Nuts and Bolts is a very useful accessory for maintaining your PC

It is difficult to summarise in a few lines everything this software is capable of doing. However, Nuts and Bolts is a complete, efficient product, useful for everyone, from the beginner to the experienced, who want to keep their PC correctly configured.

Software publisher: Network Associates (McAfee).

Test configuration: Cyrix 166, 32 Mb RAM, 1.6 Gb DD EIDE.

(© text published with the permission of the Planet Press agency
http://martignan.com/ppresse).

Index

F

Failure
  bugs 18
  in module x at address xxxx 13, 94
Failures
  black screen 15
  configuration 13
  driver 17
  general points 12
  hard disk 15
  physical failures of a PC 15
  power failure 23
  ScanDisk 42
  symptoms 12
FAT16 102
FAT32 102
Faulty sectors 42
FDISK 103
  and FAT32 mode 138
  in practice 137
  introduction 16
  /MBR command 109, 116
  partitioning 123
  virus 109, 116
File dates 59
Files
  extensions 36
  multimedia (types of) 38
  non-existent 35
  redundant 34
  system 51
  temporary 16
  temporary Internet 76
  temporary Windows 37

  unnecessary 58
  unnecessary under MS-DOS 37
  Word 36
Filing 34
Floppy disk drives, cleaning 30
FORMAT (command) 140
Formatting 16
  factory 134
  basic 134, 135
  software 140
Fragmentation, minimising the risks 41
Fragmentation risks 41

G

Garbage 36
gif extension 38
Graphics performance 145
GSM, effect on the PC 31

H

Hard disk
  congested 28
  formatting 16
  malfunction 16
  principles 15
Hard disk light 15
History of the PC 10
Housekeeping, the defragmenter 40